EXPLORING COPING AND ADAPTATION IN VETERAN ARMY NURSES WITH

COMBAT-RELATED POST-TRAUMATIC STRESS DISORDER

by

Thelma Nicholls

Copyright 2016

A Dissertation Presented in Partial Fulfillment
of the Requirements for the Degree
Doctor of Philosophy in Nursing

University of Phoenix

The Dissertation Committee for Thelma Nicholls certifies approval
of the following dissertation:

EXPLORING COPING AND ADAPTATION IN VETERAN ARMY
NURSES WITH COMBAT-RELATED POST-TRAUMATIC STRESS DISORDER

Committee: Judith Treschuk, PhD, Chair

                       Jeanie Bachand, PhD, Committee Member

                       Cydney Mullen, PhD, Committee Member

Judith V. Treschuk
Judith Treschuk

Jeanie Bachand
Jeanie Bachand

Cydney K. Mullen
Cydney Mullen

Jeremy Moreland
Jeremy Moreland, PhD
Academic Dean, School of Advanced Studies
University of Phoenix

Date Approved: March 7, 2016

Copyright © 2017 Thelma Nicholls
Copyright © 2017 ASPECT Books, Inc.
ISBN-13: 978-1-4796-0869-0 (Paperback)
Library of Congress Control Number: 2017916546

AB **ASPECT Books**
www.ASPECTBooks.com

ABSTRACT

This research study explored coping and adaptation in veteran army nurses with combat-related Post Traumatic Stress Disorder (PTSD). A qualitative case study method was used to explore coping and adaption in veteran army nurses with combat-related PTSD, and how coping with PTSD affects the concepts of self, the role of self in relation to others, and personal relationships in this cohort of army nurses. A directed content analysis based upon the Roy Adaptation Model (RAM) conceptualization of coping and adaptation was used to analyze the study data. Use of purposeful and snowball sampling method yielded 14 study participants that were either in active duty, retired or separated from active duty status, and who met all other inclusion criteria. Validation of PTSD was accomplished using the PTSD Check List-Military Version (PCL-M). A pilot study with three veteran army nurses with combat-related PTSD and who met the inclusion criteria was used to test interview questions prior to the main study. Analysis of data from the semi-structured interviews was completed with the assistance of NVivo 10 to determine prominent patterns for interpretation. Three themes emerged from data: Strategies for coping and adapting, Poor self-concept, and Relationship challenges. Study findings revealed that veteran army nurses with combat-related PTSD were at the compensatory adaptation level based on the concepts of the theoretical framework. The findings also indicated that veteran army nurses with combat-related PTSD need more targeted assistance and support to employ effective coping and adaptation strategies.

DEDICATION

To God be the glory, for to whom much is given, much is required. This study is dedicated to my husband Robert for his support and encouragement when I felt like giving up; for being the wind beneath my wings and for believing in me. You were content to let me shine. To my mother, my sons Gavin, Gary, and Gregory; my grandchildren Kacey, Kyree, Makhi, Courtney, Gabby, Jazlyn and Tyler, all for whom I strive daily to be a role model. Finally, to my darling Maltese, Max who was my companion many days and nights when everyone else was asleep.

ACKNOWLEDGEMENTS

My deepest appreciation to those who agreed to participate in this study. The brave men and women of the Army Nurse Corps who behind the scenes save lives every minute of every day. Thank you. Without you this study would not have been possible. Achieving this doctoral degree would not be possible without the wonderful team that I was blessed with. To Dr. Treschuk. Thank you for being more than my committee chairperson. You were my mentor. You encouraged me to keep persevering and to see the light at the end of the tunnel. To my committee members Dr. Mullen and Dr. Bachand, the guidance you provided was invaluable. As a team, you all were able to make sense out of words that were somewhat incoherent to me at times. Thank you all.

TABLE OF CONTENTS

Contents   Page

LIST OF TABLES

LIST OF FIGURES

Chapter 1

Introduction and Overview

Just like moons and like suns,
With the certainty of tides,
Just like hopes springing high,
Still I'll rise.
—Maya Angelou (1978)

War is not a new phenomenon for Americans. The 1700s included the

Revolutionary War, which was followed in the 1800s by the War of 1812, the Mexican

War, the Civil War, and the Spanish-American War. In the 1900s, millions of Americans

were affected by World Wars I and II, the Korean War, the Vietnam War, and the Persian

Gulf War (Defense Casualty Analysis System, 2013). Despite this history of war, the

attacks on September 11, 2001, significantly changed the U.S. military's strategic focus

from seeking international peace and reconciliation to defending against terrorism

("9/11," 2011). In 2001, America's leaders launched a global war on terrorism,

beginning with Operation Enduring Freedom (OEF), continuing with Operation Iraqi

Freedom (OIF), and then Operation New Dawn (OND) (Defense Casualty Analysis

System, 2013).

To support America's war efforts, some service members, including nurses,

undergo multiple and sometimes lengthy deployments. In preparation for deployment,

service members attend extensive training programs away from home, during which they

pass through several stages of the emotional cycle of deployment (Deployment Health

and Family Readiness Library, 2006). Seven stages of the emotional cycle can cause or

amplify stress and turmoil: (a) expecting deployment, (b) disconnecting and distancing

self from others, (c) struggling with emotional ineptitude, (d) regaining some stability, (e) anticipating his or her homecoming, (f) readjusting and reprocessing, and (g) recovering and stabilizing. The first three stages can have profound effects on the psyches of service members who are deployed multiple times, potentially leading to PTSD (Deployment Health and Family Readiness Library, 2006).

Post-traumatic stress disorder (PTSD) is a condition of persistent emotional stress resulting from experiencing or witnessing one or more traumatic events, and is considered one of the most common psychiatric illnesses among war veterans (American Psychiatric Association [APA], 2013). Individuals who suffer from PTSD exhibits symptoms from each of four symptom clusters The first symptom cluster is intrusion, in which the individual experiences involuntary memories, traumatic nightmares, and flashbacks. The second cluster is avoidance, which might manifest through depression, panic attacks, and emotional numbness. The third cluster is negative alterations in thoughts and mood, which often involves blaming self or others for the event, feeling alienated, or feeling uninterested in activities previously enjoyed. The final cluster is alterations in arousal and reactivity, such as having problems sleeping and concentrating, being hypervigilant, and being irritable (APA, 2013).

Approximately 20% of Iraq and Afghanistan veterans have PTSD and/or Depression. As of September 2014 there are approximately 2.7 million American veterans of the Iraq and Afghanistan wars (Department of Veterans Affairs, 2015). PTSD statistics are fluid, and are reviewed over time for veterans. Identifying a more up-to-date and accurate number is difficult. For example, an undocumented number of army nurses, a subcategory of service members in the Iraq/Afghanistan conflicts, have been diagnosed with combat-associated PTSD. For fiscal years 2003–2011, there were 6,555 active duty nurses in the army, 66% of whom were female. During this timeframe, 43% of females were deployed, versus 65% of males (Defense Manpower Data Center, 2013). This ratio is relevant because Feczer and Bjorklund (2009) suggested possible gender bias by the Veterans Affairs (VA) health care system when diagnosing PTSD. Benda and House (2003) discovered that only 19.8% of the 40.1% females who met PTSD criteria were diagnosed with the disorder. In comparison, 59.1% of the 62.7% males who met the criteria for PTSD were diagnosed. Pereira (2002) obtained similar results from conducting a study involving veterans of the Vietnam and Persian Gulf Wars. The results indicate that though the symptoms of PTSD are the same for male and female veterans, male veterans were more likely to receive a diagnosis of PTSD than were female veterans.

Chapter 1 of this qualitative case study provides insight into the background, problem, purpose, significance, nature, questions, and theoretical framework of the study. A focus on the problem of coping and adaptation of veteran army nurses with combat-related PTSD explores and identifies methods of coping and adaptation that emerged from the perspective of the experiences of 14 veteran army nurses with combat-related PTSD who have been deployed in support of the Global War on Terrorism (GWOT).

Background of the Problem

Every day, nurses provide care to patients, sometimes in extremely stressful situations, and nurses are often exposed to varying degrees of trauma, which are characterized as professional hazards. For the army nurse, providing care is compounded by the additional variables of deployment, challenges of the combat environment, and exposure to horrific human suffering. The human body can demonstrate resiliency after traumatic events; however, the physical, mental, and emotional consequences of war can be severe even for the most resilient person. Exposure to trauma increases psychological stress, which leads to distress and psychiatric illnesses such as PTSD (Ursano, Fullerton, Weisaeth, & Raphael, 2007).

PTSD is an emergent health care issue, one that has significantly plagued the military population. Kulka et al. (1988) reported 15% of veterans had PTSD and 31% were likely to develop PTSD in their lifetimes. The results of more recent research show that 12–13% of service members screen positive for PTSD within three to four months after deployment, and up to 17% screen positive 12 months after deployment. Further, of the veterans who accessed the VA health systems during the Iraq conflicts between 2002 and 2008, 21.8% were diagnosed with PTSD. As the wars continued, the number of service members diagnosed with PTSD increased significantly (Hoge & Castro, 2005; Seal et al., 2009).

In 2004, Major General Gale Pollock, 22nd Chief of the U.S. Army Nurse Corps, made several tours through the country (Boivin, 2005). Her goal was to hear firsthand the experiences of individuals suffering from PTSD. During a military medical conference in November 2004, Pollock addressed an audience of army nurses and acknowledged that PTSD was as much a real and present concern for the military as the condition had been a generation before (Boivin, 2005).

In an interview with Boivin (2005), Major General Pollock emphasized it is normal for soldiers to experience emotional reactions to the trauma of combat and that suppressing emotional reactions can contribute to long-term, disabling PTSD. Furthermore, Pollock declared that the global war on terrorism had transformed the army, requiring nurses in the Army Nurse Corps to adopt a warrior mind-set to survive in hostile situations. In March 2005, approximately 2,000 nurses were deployed to support of the war on terrorism, and the average length of deployment was 1 year (Boivin, 2005).

Problem Statement

The general problem is that military service personnel deployed to a combat zone are subjected to mental and physical stress regardless of their roles in the mission. For some, the physical and mental stress begins at predeployment training, continues throughout the deployment, and even continues post deployment (Hoge, Auchterlonie, & Milliken, 2006; King, King, Vogt, Knight, & Samper, 2006; Wilgus, 2011). Because military personnel are responsible for protecting American citizens, the personnel must develop resiliency to overcome both physical and psychological traumas. This principle applies to members of the Army Nurse Corps because military nurses are subjected to extreme demands in combat zones (Wilgus, 2011). For instance, army nurses are under significant mental demands to care for the seriously wounded in a timely manner on the battlefield. These nurses must multitask while in a persistent state of heightened awareness.

Researchers have conducted a plethora of studies on PTSD among military service members, including in relation to gender and other demographic variables (Nayback, 2009). The specific problem for the study is the gap in the literature concerning how active duty, retired, and separated veteran army nurses cope and adapt while living with combat-related PTSD. Recent studies have been focused on nurses in general, including civilian nurses and licensed practical nurses. Further, PTSD and resiliency have been examined in regard to soldiers as a group, which includes army nurses, civilian nurses working in military treatment facilities, licensed practical nurses, and combat medics (Phillips, 2011; U.S. Army, 2010; Weidlich, Ugarriza, & Doris, 2015).

Research is needed on active duty, retired, and separated veteran army nurses with combat-related PTSD to understand how this specific group copes and adapts when experiencing PTSD. Without this research, it is unclear whether and how veteran army nurses with combat-related PTSD cope and adapt. For those veteran nurses who continue to provide care for other service members, it is possible they may be vicariously reliving the trauma of war. It is imperative to understand how veteran army nurses with combat-related PTSD cope and adapt to living with PTSD, especially those who continue to provide care to other service members and their families. The results of this research may indicate the need to refocus treatment modalities across all branches of the military.

Purpose Statement

The purpose of this qualitative case study was to explore how veteran army nurses diagnosed with combat-related PTSD cope and adapt. To understand the concepts of coping and adapting in this specific population, the theory of Roy's adaptation model (RAM) was used. To achieve the purpose of the study, interviews were conducted with 14 veteran army nurses who have or had combat-related PTSD and who lived in the southwestern United States. The semi-structured interviews contained open-ended questions that elicited detailed responses from the participants. The data were analyzed via content analysis (Appendix A) to uncover several emerging themes.

Significance of the Study

Nurses strive to promote health and wellness through caring, which is the essence of nursing and the focus of nursing practice. Every day brings new emotional and psychological challenges for nurses as they enter into covenant relationships with patients. Nurses are effectively positioned to help individuals who are experiencing significant stressors and strains to improve or recover from their distress through interpersonal connections. By establishing these connections, nurses can empower individuals to find and employ effective coping and adaptation skills (Roy, 2009). Morrison and Korol (2014) discussed the possible depletion of empathy and compassion in nurses, especially those close to trauma. Researching coping and adaptation of veteran army nurses with combat-related PTSD could enrich nursing knowledge by using and building on data from the study, and ultimately lead to helping military service members cope and adapt with PTSD.

The research study is significant for leadership and nursing. The insights gained from the results of this study have potential to be of significance to leaders of Medical Command, military services, the Veteran Administration (VA), and nursing organizations. The findings do indicate the need to develop and implement strategies to provide specialized mental health services to veteran army nurses experiencing combat-related PTSD. Finally, the study findings have the potential to provide a foundation for successful coping and adaptation in veteran nurses from all branches of the military, as well as other service members.

Nature of the Study

Qualitative methodology and case study design were used for the research. The methodology was chosen as an appropriate way to explore the phenomena of coping and adaptation in the population of veteran army nurses with combat-related PTSD. Qualitative research places emphasis on the universal and individual characteristics of the human experience (Vivar, 2007). The qualitative method was appropriate for uncovering the complexities of a phenomenon through acquiring extensive data (Strauss & Corbin, 2008). Using the qualitative method in the study resulted in ample description of the intricacies of human resiliency in military nurses.

Overview of the Research Method

The data in qualitative research are textual rather than numerical, as in quantitative research; thus, qualitative data are not statistically analyzed but are textually examined to understand the meanings of the responses (Strauss & Corbin, 2008). The theoretical background of qualitative research relates to the humanistic approach, in which the goal is to examine how individuals observe reality. This research method corresponds with the theoretical postulations of RAM where the personal encounters of the individual are captured and recounted from that person's perspective (Perrett, 2007). Using quantitative methodologies was inappropriate for this study because this approach involves quantifying variables and measurements, as well as applying statistical tests (Hoe & Hoare, 2013). With quantitative research, the investigator is detached from the participants. By contrast, in qualitative research the investigator interacts with participants within their social and cultural environment (Lincoln & Guba, 1990).

Denzin and Lincoln (2008) encouraged qualitative researchers to emphasize the structured nature of reality in a social context, the intimate rapport between the researcher and the topic, and the conditional restrictions that shape inquiry. Qualitative researchers pursue answers to questions relating to social experiences and how those experiences are given meaning. The quantitative method is different from the goal of this study, which was to explore the unique, personal experiences of how veteran army nurses with combat-related PTSD cope and adapt. To reduce participants to the level of statistical numbers is to overlook the uniqueness of the participants' experiences. A credulous relationship between the researcher and participant influenced the therapeutic benefits of the interviews for the participants, as well as increases the richness of the data (Murray, 2003).

Overview of Design and Appropriateness

The case study design was appropriate for the study because the objective of the study was to explore how veteran army nurses cope and adapt with combat-related PTSD. The case study design was also appropriate because all participants were selected from one case (James, 2013), namely nurses with combat-related PTSD who lived around a military base in the southwestern United States.

A single case or multiple cases can be the focus of case study research. The single-case focus was more appropriate than the multi-case focus for the study because all participants were members of the same bounded system (Yin, 2009, 2012). The multi-case approach involves examining multiple groups with distinct qualities and bounded systems (Baxter & Jack, 2008; Houghton, Casey, Shaw, & Murphy, 2013). The focus of the multi-case design is on contrasting the groups (Baxter & Jack, 2008). The focus of the study was not on contrasting different cases of coping and adaptation with PTSD. Therefore, the single-case design was appropriate for the study.

Other qualitative designs did not align with the objective of the study. For instance, the ethnographic design was not selected because the focus of this design is to explore features of a culture, such as actions, beliefs, and languages (Pensoneau-Conway, & Toyosaki, 2011). Participants in the study were not limited to one cultural group; consequently, this design was inappropriate for the study. Grounded theory design was also inappropriate for the study because the objective of grounded theory is the development of a theory about the phenomenon studied (Charmaz, 2006). The study is founded on RAM, and the intent was not to develop a new theory, though the results of the study might validate or extend the concepts of RAM. The phenomenological design was not chosen because the intent of this design is to understand the lived experiences of individuals from their perspective (Moustakas, 1994).

Research Questions

Three research questions were used to guide the study and to achieve the purpose of the study, which was to explore how veteran army nurses diagnosed with combat-related PTSD cope and adapt. The research questions were:

RQ1: How are veteran nurses coping and adapting after being diagnosed with combat-related PTSD?

RQ2: From the perspective of effective adaptation, what does coping and adapting with PTSD mean for veteran nurses?

RQ3: How does coping with PTSD affect the concept of self, the role of self in relation to others, and personal relationships?

Theoretical Framework

Roy's Adaptation Model was used as the theoretical framework for exploring coping and adaptation of veteran army nurses with combat-related PTSD. This model provided a value-centered perspective for recognizing issues for scholarly inquiry. The model's concepts provide several methods for researchers to develop unified knowledge of the health of people as individuals and groups (Roy, 2011a).

Overview of RAM

Sister Callista Roy developed RAM in the 1960s by building on the ideas of experts in other disciplines. A fundamental concept in RAM is adaptation, and the concept is based on both scientific and philosophical assumptions that Roy developed during her career. The scientific assumptions related to Bertalanffy's general systems theory and Helson's adaptation-level theory (Roy, 2009). The philosophical assumptions are rooted in the general principles of humanism, cosmic unity, and veritivity. Roy introduced the concept of veritivity in 1988 to introduced the idea that all firmly established knowledge is related (Roy, 2009). Roy (1988) defined veritivity as "a principle of human nature that affirms a common purposefulness of human existence" (p.30). As Roy used new knowledge about other cultures and the origins of the universe, the model evolved and Roy developed a new philosophical concept called cosmic unity. Through the concept of cosmic unity, Roy (2009) emphasized that people and the earth share similar patterns and relationships.

Humans are seen as a unitary adaptive system involving components of the body, mind, and spirit working together as a whole. When one of the components is out of alignment, the individual has to find ways to adjust and adapt to remain functional. Roy (2009) theorized that humans adjust to, and affect their environments through thinking and feeling.

Coping and Adaptation Processing

Coping and adaptation processes are intrinsic or learned habits of interrelating with, recognizing, or reacting to a stimulus in the changing environment. These innate or acquired coping processes are categorized as the regulator and the cognator subsystem (Roy, 2009). The regulator subsystem responds to internal and external stimuli through physiologic channels, whilst the cognator subsystem responds through cognitive-emotional channels. The individual uses the emotions to develop defenses that are used to find relief from anxiety and to make emotional judgements.

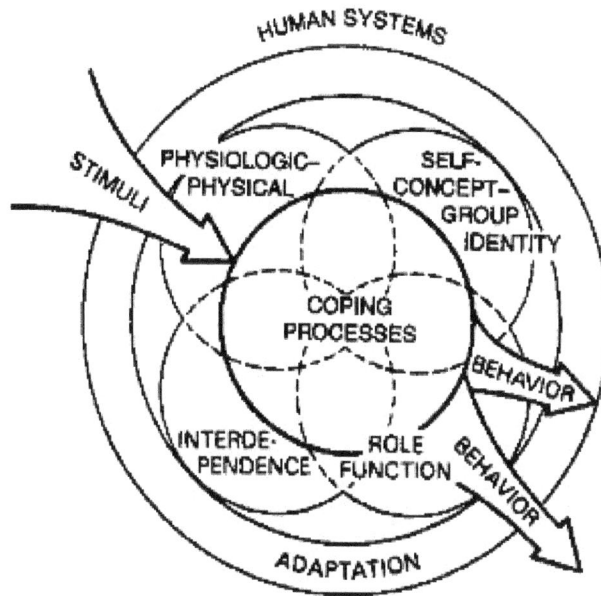

Figure 1. Diagrammatic representation of the human adaptation system.
Reprinted with permission (Appendix B).

The ability to understand cognitive and emotional processing done by the

cognator subsystem is necessary to understand how individuals are adapting (Roy,

2009). Cognitive processing is essential to devise a planned response to a stimuli (Roy,

2011a), and the process of devising that plan is managed by the cognator (2009). From

this perspective Roy developed a middle range theory of coping and adaptation (Figure 2)

to demonstrate the phases of cognitive processing. Roy combined the four adaptive

modes with the middle range theory of cognitive processing, which resulted in a middle

range theory of coping and adaptation processing (Roy, 2011a).

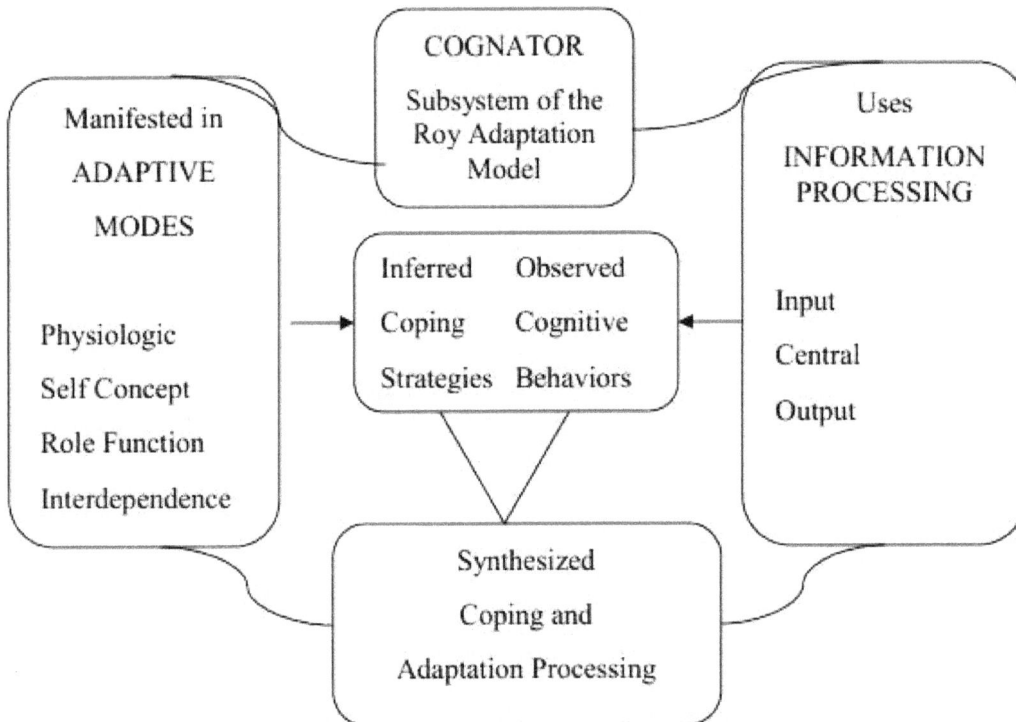

Figure 2. Middle-range theory of coping and adaptation.
Reprinted with permission (Appendix C).

Roy (2009) discussed three types of stimuli in the environment that impacts the

human adaptive system: focal, contextual, and residual stimuli. The focal-stimulus is the

internal or external force that an individual focuses on. It is not the medical diagnosis.

The focal stimuli in this study were the symptoms of PTSD. Contextual stimuli are other

environmental influence that exist alongside the focal stimulus but are not the

individual's focus. Contextual stimuli are all other factors present in the situation that

influences the effect of the focal stimuli. Contextual stimuli influences coping efforts.

(Roy, 2009). In this study, the contextual stimuli were combat experiences, spirituality,

support systems, and social demographics (age, sex, gender, etc.). Residual stimuli are

unclear environmental factors contributing to the situation. In a nursing environment residual stimuli are often a guess or intuition based on the nurses' knowledge or past experiences with clients with similar problems (Roy, 2009). For the purpose of this study, residual stimuli were combined with contextual stimuli.

Adaptive Modes.

The functioning of control processes, such as the regulator and the stabilizer subsystems, cannot be observed directly. Consequently, Roy (2009) developed four adaptive modes that researchers could use to observe behaviors and thereby understand the control processes. As displayed in (Figure 1), the four adaptive modes are physiologic, self-concept, role function, and interdependence. Roy initially developed the modes for individuals but later expanded the modes to include groups. For the purpose of this study, the modes were discussed as they pertain to individuals.

Physiologic mode. The human body is composed of physiological systems, such as the nervous system, cardiac system, and respiratory system, which manifest in behaviors that indicate the body's physiologic integrity. A person has physiologic integrity when his or her physical needs are met (Roy, 2009).

Self-concept mode. An individual's perceptions of self and others' reactions form the self-concept. In RAM, the physical and personal selves are components of the self-concept mode of the individual, which is described as a complex group of ideas and principles that a person embraces about self at a certain time (Roy, 2009). Self-concept integrity is achieved when individuals' psychic and spiritual needs are met, giving them a sense of unity, meaning, and purposefulness in the universe Roy (2009).

Role-function mode. The role-function mode has an emphasis on the individual's role in society. The process of understanding and accepting the societal role is called social integrity. Social integrity is the fundamental need in the role-function mode. Social integrity is essential for the individual to understand self as it relates to others because this understanding and acceptance define behavior responses (Roy, 2009).

Interdependence mode. The focus of the interdependence mode is on relationships between individuals, including interactions that involve communicating love, value, and importance. The fundamental desire in this mode is interpersonal reliability, or security in relations. Relational integrity is achieved through obtaining adequate affection, development, and resources (Roy, 2009).

Adaptation levels.

The four adaptive modes are used to understand human behaviors and levels of adaptation (Roy, 2009). Within the four adaptive modes the three levels of adaptation identified by Roy are:

Integrated adaptation level. At the integrated coping level, the individual is effectively meeting the challenges brought on by the stimuli.

Compensatory adaptation level. Coping at the compensatory level is an indication that the individual is partially able to meet the challenges brought on by the stimuli, and has developed ways to compensate.

Compromised adaptation level. Individuals who are at a compromised adaptation level are unable to compensate or to achieve integrated adaptation (Roy, 2009). When faced with a focal or contextual stimulus, the best outcome is for the individual to respond at the integrated or compensatory level (Roy, 2009). Antai-Otong

(2008) described this response as the concept of health, in terms of mental well-being, and not absence of illness. As indicated in RAM, being healthy depends on whether the person is adapting effectively in order to become integrated and whole.

Theoretical Assumptions

According to Roy's theoretical assumptions, when researchers use the RAM as a framework, they should focus on coping, adaptation, and signs that indicate when people are adapting effectively. Understanding these signs can help researchers discover how people are defined by their ability to adapt (Perrett, 2007). Another assumption of RAM is that the phenomenon under study directly relates to humans; in the study, the phenomenon is PTSD. Another essential assumption is that the problem is related to life patterns and coping with health and illness. The problem in this study was whether veteran army nurses were coping with, and adapting to combat-related PTSD, and how they were coping with and adapting to PTSD. The last RAM assumption is related to enhancing adaptive coping, such as how nurses adapt in relation to the dimensions of the model's four adaptive modes.

Definition of Terms

Defining terms used in a study helps to clarify meanings and fosters mutual interpretation of the concepts involved in the study.

Acquired coping processes are strategies the individual learns for managing stimuli (Roy, 2009).

Adaptation is how people, individually or in groups, consciously change themselves to fit effectively into social groups and their environment (Roy, 2009).

Adaptation level is the degree to which a person adapts to meet the challenges of the environment. The levels are described as integrated, compensatory, and compromised (Roy, 2009).

Adaptive behavior demonstrates reactions that support the integrity of the human adaptive system (Roy, 2009).

Army nurses are registered nurses who have at least a bachelor's degree in nursing and who are serving in the army (U.S. Army, 2014).

Army Nurse Corps is a special medical branch of the Army Medical Department (2014).

Cognator subsystem is a person's cognitive coping process, which involves interpretation and processing of information, understanding, wisdom, and feeling (Roy, 2009).

Combat Medic is a health care specialist with the Military Occupational Specialty code of 68W

Compensatory process is one of three adaptation levels at which the person's cognitive and physiological coping mechanisms are activated to meet the challenging needs of the environment (Roy, 2009).

Compromised process is the level at which the individual fails to meet the challenges brought on by the environment (Roy, 2009).

Coping processes are inherent or learned ways of reacting to the fluctuating environment (Roy, 2009).

Coping and adaptation processing is the designing of innate and acquired ways of absorbing, managing, and responding to a changing environment in everyday and critical situations that guides behavior toward survival and growth (Roy, 2011a).

Effective adaptation is a positive behavior demonstrated by an individual that indicate the individual is at the integrated coping level (Roy, 2009).

Human adaptive system is an aggregate system with subsystems that function together for a purpose. (Roy, 2009).

Humanism is the philosophical and psychological movement that indicates the personal and individual elements of the human experience that are fundamental to understanding and respecting (Roy, 2009).

Innate coping processes are those traits that are genetically determined (Roy, 2009).

Ineffective behavior is a response that disrupts the integrated life process of the adaptive system (Roy, 2009).

Integrated life process is the adjustment level where there is unification of the structures and operations of the subsystems, creating a stable process to meet environmental needs (Roy, 2009).

Regulator subsystem is the physiological coping mechanism through which the body regulates the neural, chemical, and endocrine systems in an attempt to adapt (Roy, 2009).

Reservists are service members serving in the Reserve component of military branches.

System is a combination of different parts coming together for the same purpose (Roy, 2009).

Veritivity is a belief that existence of humanity is a shared purpose (Roy, 2009).

Veteran army nurses are registered nurses who were deployed to a combat area or discharged from active duty for a service connected disability.

Assumptions

The first assumption was recruitment of participants might have been difficult because of the sensitive nature of the research topic, and the negative connotations attached to mental health issues. The purposive sampling method initially yielded seven participants. Application of the snowball sampling approach yielded an additional nine participants. The second assumption was that participants would agree to disclose a diagnosis of PTSD. Participants agreed and self-disclosed their diagnosis of PTSD, as well as acknowledged the diagnosis on the demographic questionnaire (Appendix D). Validation of PTSD was accomplished using the military version of the PTSD checklist (PCL-M) (Appendix E). The PCL-M is a 17-item standardized self-report rating scale based on the DSM-IV criteria for PTSD. Participants were asked to respond to the questions as they did when they were first diagnosed with PTSD. Responses options and assigned points are from 1 ("not at all") to 5 ("Extremely"). When tabulated, a score of 50 or more is indicative of a probable diagnosis of combat-related PTSD. The tool has good test-retest reliability and validity (Wilkins, Lang, & Norman, 2011). Both the questionnaire and checklist were accessed through Survey Monkey. The third assumption was that participants would be honest and forthcoming with their responses to the interview questions (Appendix

F). Because it was not possible to objectively assess participants' honesty, each interview was done in a private room at a local library to create an environment where where they would feel free to disclose information. Participants were repeatedly reminded of the confidentiality agreement (Appendix G) and they were urged to respond candidly to the interview questions.

Throughout the interview process participants were encouraged to ask for clarification of any question or information of which they were unsure. When necessary, they were asked to expound on ambiguous responses. The fourth assumption was the use of open-ended questions in semi-structured interviews would result in detailed, extensive data. The semi-structured interviews and open-ended questions provided participants fluidity in their responses, which took different paths as determined by the information provided by each participant. This approach resulted in the richness of data received for the study. The final assumption was that individuals would become more aware of the experiences that affect their life choices. This assumption was based on the principle of humanism within the RAM. In humanism individuals demonstrates purposeful behaviors, and struggles to preserve integrity and to realize the need for relationships (Roy, 1988). Because it was not possible to objectively assess the outcome of this assumption, awareness was through acknowledging, resulting in participants becoming more aware.

Scope

The scope of this research study focused on exploring coping and adaptation in veteran army nurses with combat-related PTSD. The study was confined to in-depth semi-structured interviews with a purposeful snowball sample of 14 veteran army nurses with combat-related PTSD who specifically served in either Operation Iraqi Freedom, Operation Enduring Freedom, or Operation New Dawn (OIF, OEF, OND) conflict and had or have combat-related PTSD. The location of the study was restricted to individuals living within a 30-mile radius of a military base in the southwestern United States. The scope of the study included male and female participants who were active duty, retired, or separated from the Army. By necessity, the gathering of data required the honest input of individuals who were willing to participate in the study.

Limitations

Causal interpretations cannot be made from case studies because alternative accounts cannot be ruled out. This methodology involves the behavior of one person, group, or organization, and may or may not reflect the behavior of similar people. Case studies can suggest what might be found in similar organization, but further research would be needed to verify whether the findings from one study would generalize elsewhere (Delva, Kirby, Knapper, & Birthwhistle, 2002). This qualitative case study was limited because of the sample size. The small sample of 14 participants limited the generalizability of the findings. Though results of the study might be applicable to combat medics in the army and registered nurses in other branches of the military who have been deployed in support of either of the conflicts or all the conflicts, the findings of

22

the research study might not be generalized to nurses in other branches of the military in who were never deployed.

Another potential limitation was researcher bias, which might have reduced the credibility of the findings. Personal biases might have been an issue in this study because the researcher is a veteran army nurse with combat-related PTSD. Safeguards were implemented to prevent personal biases and to promote credibility and dependability. To safeguard against potential biases, the researcher, through personal journaling (Appendix H), reflected on personal values, biases, and assumptions. Field notes were examined and critiqued by peer reviewers to determine potential biases.

Delimitations

The delimitations of a study provide boundaries and can also reduce transferability of the findings to other groups, times, and contexts (Lincoln & Guba, 1990). The first delimitation of the study was the narrowed focus on coping and adaptation from the perspective of veteran army nurses with combat-related PTSD. Another delimitation concerned the sampling method. Purposive sampling followed by snowball sampling was used to select participants who met the sample criteria; the criteria were established to help ensure rich data could be gathered from individuals with in-depth experience regarding coping and adapting with PTSD. Experiencing combat is specific to the military and victims of war; therefore, combat-related PTSD is specific to this group of individuals (Koenen, Stellman, Sommer, & Stellman, 2008). Sampling these individuals had the largest potential for a greater understanding of coping and adapting with combat-related PTSD.

Summary

Chapter 1 was a presentation of the background of the problem, the problem statement, and the purpose statement. The chapter also included discussion of the significance of the study, the nature of the study, the research questions, and the theoretical framework. Definitions of relevant terms were also discussed. Finally, assumptions, scope of the study, limitations, and delimitations of the study were presented. While there was evidence from the literature that research had been completed on PTSD as well as PTSD and healthcare providers, no study had been identified that explored coping and adaptation in veteran army nurses with combat-related PTSD. Questions in Chapter 1 assisted in expanding discoveries in Chapter 4 and creation of recommendations and conclusions in Chapter 5. Chapter 2 provided a review of the literature that guided this qualitative case study as well as supported the need for the research study.

Chapter 2

Review of the Literature

The purpose of this qualitative case study was to explore how veteran army nurses diagnosed with combat-related PTSD cope and adapt. The purpose of the literature review was to present an evaluation of studies located in the literature relative to coping and adaptation with PTSD, particularly in veteran army nurses. Chapter 2 provides a description of the search methods used as well as an historical background of PTSD and coping and adaptation. Three major themes were discovered in the literature: comorbidity and PTSD, prevalence of research using the RAM, and coping and adaption from a general perspective. Each theme is further divided into several sub-topics to categorize, explain, and demonstrate the framework used for this study, which is RAM. Following each theme is a table that displays all the research studies that were examined and reviewed for the literature. Finally, a summary of the evidence is presented to elucidate the consistencies and inconsistencies in the literature review, identification of gaps in the literature, and a conclusion of the body of evidence supporting the necessity to explore how veteran army nurses cope and adapt with combat-related PTSD.

Search Methods

To obtain evidence for this literature review, searches were conducted using the EBSCOhost database located on the University of Phoenix website. Additionally, literature was obtained and reviewed from InfoTrac, Journals@Ovid, ProQuest, ERIC, and CINAHL. Relevant search terms used were PTSD, army nurses and PTSD, army nurses with combat-related PTSD and coping, coping and adaptation, PTSD and military, effects of PTSD, effective coping and adaptation. In determining which resources to include in the literature review, preference was given to studies written in English spanning from 2000-2015. The literature review also contained foundational research and theory development from resources earlier than 2000. The themes (Table 1), emerged from the literature review were the historical background of PTSD, PTSD and other factors, the prevalence of research using RAM, the prevalence of PTSD in the military community, and coping and adaptation.

Table 1

Summary of Literature Review

Topics	Peer Reviewed Articles	Stand Alone Website
Historical Background	11	4
PTSD and other factors	14	
Prevalence of PTSD in the Military Community	3	1
Prevalence of Research Using RAM	8	
Coping and Adaptation	36	5

History of PTSD and War

For centuries, scholars have examined the effects of stress on the body. Hans Selye first discovered the effects of stress in 1935. That discovery led to what is now known as the stress response described as a psychological and biological response when individuals encounter a threat (Perdrizet 1997). In 1952, the first publication of the *Diagnostic and Statistical Manual of Mental Disorders (DSM)* published the diagnosis of PTSD under the name gross stress reaction (APA, 2014). Since then, several editions of the *DSM* were published with revised classifications of mental disorders.

It was not until 1980 that members of the APA recognized the diagnosis of PTSD which is now regarded by mental health professionals as well as the public as a mental health illness (APA, 2000). The 5th edition is most recent edition of the *DSM* published by the American Psychiatric Association and was released in 2013. In the *DSM-V* the symptoms of PTSD are divided into four clusters of symptoms whereas the previous edition carried three clusters of symptoms (Department of Veterans Affairs, 2014).

Psychological trauma leading to PTSD was not so much a discovery in 1980 as it was a rediscovery. While the name had not yet been identified, Swiss, German, French, and Spanish physicians recognized the condition of PTSD in the 16th and 17th centuries (Bentley, 2005). In 1678, Swiss military physicians coined the term *nostalgia* to refer to conditions soldiers were experiencing, including melancholy, loss of appetite, anxiety, heart palpitations, and insomnia (Bentley, 2005). These symptoms were later termed *homesickness* by German and French physicians; Spanish physicians used the term *to be broken* (Bentley, 2005).

World Wars I and II

The purpose of a country's military is to defend it from invasion and external attack. World War I (WWI) began in 1914 and over the four years of the War over 9 million soldiers died and over 20 million had some kind of injury. The method for assessing PTSD (a nervous breakdown) during the War was to determine vulnerability traits in a soldier, and mitigate those traits such as childhood experiences, genetic makeup and a soldier's personality (Pols & Oak, 2007). During this period, Thomas W. Salmon, an American psychiatrist visited Britain to survey their treatment methods for shell shock. His comprehensive report became the basis for how psychiatry was practiced in

America. One treatment method in the United States was to place soldiers on a few days bed rest after which they would quickly return to the fighting lines. This approach was taken because treatment was mostly available near casualty stations several miles behind the lines of combat, which was often staffed by MEDICS (Pols & Oak, 2007). The concept of forward psychiatry was later conceived and developed as a treatment approach for shell shock (now termed PTSD) in response to the lack of psychiatric treatments and services for soldiers in behind the lines of combat, and in a medical environment (Jones & Wessely, 2003).

When WWI was declared, only a few hundred nurses and doctors were available. In anticipation to support the medical needs of a projected 2 million soldiers, the military called for volunteers. More than 22,000 women who were either qualified through university or hospital training, volunteered to serve their country. These women were in what was known as "The Women's Army Corps" (Power, 2013). During the War, nurses were often in charge of an entire ward of more than 400 patients, but they were paid less than the salary of a private in the Army. Despite the deplorable conditions, to meet the needs of soldiers on the battlefield some of these nurses volunteered to join the mobile surgical unit, which was the most dangerous duty of all. This unit travelled directly behind the fighting men and these nurses provided first line care to hundreds of soldiers. During WWI nurses saw first-hand the effects of shell shock, and provided empathy and support to soldiers (Power, 2013).

World War II had more than 350,000 women volunteering to serve their country in the largest and most violent conflict. Of this number, approximately 60,000 registered nurses served in what is now known as the United States Army Nurse Corps, with approximately 30,000 in the combat areas (Monahan, & Neidel-Greenlee, 2004). Nurses worked in several areas of combat and were directly exposed to live fire. Despite the thousands of nurses who were in combat, and some directly behind the fighting lines, a review of the literature did not reveal any information regarding nurses and shell shock during both wars.

During both world wars PTSD was termed *battle fatigue, accident neurosis,* and *shell shock,* among others (APA, 1997). After the Vietnam War the issue of psychological trauma was brought to the forefront of public awareness. Sociopolitical movements in the 1960's resulted in a sense of liberation and openness, including discussing issues of abuse and trauma (Friedman, Keane, & Resick, 2010). Discussing these issues prompted discussion of the challenges military personnel face during deployment. Some military personnel with PTSD revealed that the war had not ended for them, but that it continued within their own minds (Friedman et al., 2010). The turning point regarding acceptance of PTSD occurred in 1980 the year the third edition of the *DSM* included a diagnostic construct of PTSD in addition to principal diagnostic criteria (APA, 2000).

Vietnam Era

In the Vietnam War, 2.8 million men and women served their country. Over the span of America's longest war then, more than 5,000 Army nurses proudly served. Nine of these nurses paid the ultimate sacrifice (Feller & Moore, 1995), as did many other service members who served in Vietnam. Although many army nurses were lonely and fearful for their safety and the safety of their patients, the nurses who served in Vietnam provided high-quality nursing care in an austere environment (West, n. d.).

In 1988, members of the Research Triangle Institute published a report on the findings from the National Vietnam Veterans' Readjustment Study (NVVRS). The purpose of the study was to find an accurate rate of incidences involving post-war psychological problems that were affecting Vietnam Veterans. A multi-method approach was used to study participants from a representative national samples of Vietnam Veterans. Study participants were individuals on active duty in the U.S. Military during the Vietnam era (Vietnam-theater veterans); individuals on active duty during the Vietnam era but not deployed to Vietnam and its borders (Vietnam-era veterans); and civilian counterparts. The results of the study revealed that 15.2% of male and 8.5% of female Vietnam War veterans had full PTSD; another 11.1% of males and 7.8% of females had partial PTSD. Individuals with partial PTSD exhibited some dysfunctional symptoms of PTSD but did not meet the full criteria listed in the *DSM* in use at that time (Kulka et al., 1988).

Civilian male participants were compared to male theater veterans on the basis of age, sex, and race or ethnicity. Civilian female participants were compared to female theater veterans on the basis of occupation. The different comparisons were selected because of the estimated 3.15 million personnel who served in Vietnam, 3.14 million were males. Of the small number of females that served most were nurses (Kulka et al., 1988). The study results did not indicate how many nurses were diagnosed with PTSD. Since this study, there has been a focus on PTSD in war veterans, but not specifically on veteran nurses with combat-related PTSD and how they cope and adapt with this illness.

Iraq and Afghanistan Conflicts

The Iraq and Afghanistan wars are extensions of the Global War on Terrorism. When compared with other wars fought by the US, the Iraq and Afghanistan wars differ in length, size, and severity. For example, the civil war was the bloodiest war fought by America. Of the 2.2 million Union soldiers, over 324,000 died. Of the 1.5 million Confederate soldiers, approximately 150,000 died. In comparison, a combined total of over 10,000 died in combat in the Iraq and Afghanistan conflicts, which is now considered America's longest war. (Department of Defense, 2007). Very little has been written about the experience of U.S. military nurses in the Iraq and Afghanistan wars. To date, two Army nurses have died in the conflicts. From the sparse up-to-date information on PTSD among the Military, it is believed that 11-20% of Veterans from the GWOT have been diagnosed with PTSD (Department of Defense, 2007). This percentage does not include those who did not report PTSD and those who seek treatments outside a military treatment facility, nor did it stipulate the percentage of nurses with PTSD (Department of Defense, 2007).

Conceptual Framework

The RAM has been applied internationally in research since the introduction of the model in 1970. The broad nature of the RAM allows it to be used in assessment of the coping process of Taiwanese families, its application in pregnant women in Turkey who were experiencing nausea and vomiting during pregnancy and coping and adaptation in liver transplant patients among others.

Prevalence of RAM in Research

Li and Shyu (2007) examined the processes by which Taiwanese families cope after an elderly family member with a hip fracture has been discharged from the hospital. The study's purpose was to develop a conceptual framework to understand the coping processes. A qualitative grounded theory approach was used to pursue the study's purpose. The researchers used the basis of RAM's group approach to examine the group in terms of coping and adaptation, focusing on the concept of interdependence, which is the fourth adaptive mode in RAM. Using the purposive sampling method, Li and Shyu (2007) identified and selected eight families that included 12 caregivers and eight care receivers to participate in the study. Average age of the caregiver participants was 49.5 years. Eight of the 12 caregivers were women; three of the 12 were spouses, and the other nine were adult children. Of the eight care receiver participants, four were men. Average age of the care receiver participants was 69.6 years.

Care receivers had various health issues. One had diabetes, one was receiving renal dialysis for renal failure, and three suffered from hypertension. Diagnosis in the remaining three care receivers was not presented. However, one care receiver participant required assistance with four activities of daily living (ADLs); two required help with three ADLs, and five required assistance with two ADLs. The specifics of the ADLs requirements were not discussed. Face-to-face interviews were conducted separately with participants after receipt of tape-recorded verbal consents. A total of 44 interviews were conducted with participants one and three months post discharge. The researchers used constant comparison to analyze the data.

Study results indicated that from the perspective of RAM interdependence mode, the relationship between a caregiver and a care receiver was in harmony only when both adjust their behaviors, attitudes, and expectations. Both groups of participants maintained harmonious relationships between themselves in order to adapt to environmental changes during the post discharge timeframe. According to Li and Shyu (2007), harmony in interdependent relationships is affected by both internal and external stimuli, resulting in three family coping styles: instrumental, expressive, and distancing. Maintaining harmony was a core concept in the coping measures of the Taiwanese families when caring for an elderly relative. A three-part conceptual framework was developed from the study results. The three parts were: (1) elements that contributed to a harmonious relationship within interdependence relationships, (2) coping styles of families, and (3) different products of adaptation. The investigators proposed that the findings of the study empirically supported RAM concept of interdependence. Limitations of the study were sampling strategy and length of follow-up period.

Another study was conducted by Isbir and Mete (2013), to explore the application of RAM in pregnant women experiencing nausea and vomiting during pregnancy. The researchers' intent was to determine the effectiveness of RAM in describing the experiences of pregnant Turkish women with nausea and vomiting. The qualitative

33

exploratory study consisted of 35 participants who visited a Turkish antenatal care outpatient clinic. All 35 participants were married and in their 12 weeks of gestation with no comorbidities. Participant's mean age was 28.03. Thirty-seven percent of participants graduated high school, and at the time of the study, 54.2% of the women studied reported the pregnancy as their first.

The researchers collected data through semi-structured interviews using semi-structured questions that were developed based on the four modes of RAM. Data was also collected from participants' demographic sheets. The interviews were conducted and transcribed in Turkish and later translated into English. Data were analyzed, using the directed content analysis approach, with RAM as the theoretical framework. The researchers categorized the data into the four adaptive modes of RAM. Results of the study revealed that the stimuli triggering nausea and vomiting in the pregnant women varied by participants and that each participant responded differently to the stimuli. An understanding of humans require the determination of their individuality, which is important when providing nursing care (Isbir and Mete, 2013). This argument corresponds with Roy's (2009) argument that stimuli affect human responses. The researchers proposed that pregnant women with nausea and vomiting should be evaluated on the basis of their responses and the stimuli contributing to the responses. Limitations of the study were generalizability, cultural variability in response to different stimuli, and the use of purposive sample.

Another example of the RAM being used internationally is a research study done in Turkey. Ordin, Karayurt, and Wellard, (2013) conducted a qualitative descriptive study to explore how liver transplant patients were adapting after the transplant. Roy's adaptation model guided the study. A total of 21 participants were recruited using purposive sampling. The sample consisted of 16 males and five females in the age range of 19 to 61. The researchers intended to use focus groups for data collection. However, only one focus group interview was done with seven participants. Data were collected from the remaining 14 participants using semi-structured interviews and seven open-ended questions. Data were coded using deductive content analysis and participants' responses were catalogued according to the four modes of adaptation in the Model. The research findings were indicative of both effective and ineffective adaptation in the participants. Study results were discussed within the four adaptive modes of the RAM.

The experiences of military service members are different for every individual regardless of the branch of military or duty status. Looper (2012) conducted a qualitative secondary analysis to gain an understanding of the coping and adaptation processes of army reservist soldiers and a family member during their first year postdeployment to Iraq. A second focus was to extend or validate the RAM and the Coping and Adaptation Processing Scale (CAPS), an instrument that was derived from Roy's middle range theory of coping in human systems. The intent of the study was to determine patterns of coping and adaptation, and which contextual stimuli affected participants' ability to cope with, and manage redeployment and reunification.

The study consisted of 20 army reservists and their families. Using the RAM as its concepts of coping and adaption as the theoretical framework, the researcher used a directed content analysis approach to analyze data from 75 semi-structured interviews. There were several major findings in this study, (a) reintegration is different for each person and is longer than what previous literature suggested, (b) contextual stimuli

35

substantially influenced focal stimuli, and (c) support for the concepts of RAM and the CAPS.

One role of nursing is to educate patients and families whether the nurses are in or out of the clinical settings. Afrasiabifar, Karimi, and Hassani (2013) did a study to examine the effectiveness of a RAM-based education on adaptation of hemodialysis patients with the aim of improving the adaptation processes in hemodialysis patients. The quantitative semi-experimental study was done with 59 participants who had end-stage renal disease. A total of 64 patients were referred to the hemodialysis clinic of a hospital in Iran. Five patients were excluded for not meeting eligibility criteria, which included ages 18 to 75, no cognitive impairment or handicap, and the ability to read and write. The convenience sampling method was used to select the 59 participants who were randomly divided into two groups of test and control. Thirty-one participants made up the test group of 16 males and 15 females with a mean age of 48. The control group consisted of 28 participants with 15 males and 13 females and a mean age of 47.

Participants' behaviors and stimuli were assessed based on the RAM concepts of physiological, self-concept, role-function, and interdependence modes. The results led to the development and implementation of a nursing education plan that was executed over an eight-week period with eight one-hour sessions. The plan was evaluated two months after the eight-weeks, and the results compared with the pre-education data. To collect data the researchers used a questionnaire with demographic variables and questions divided into the four modes of the RAM. The physiological mode was assessed with 25 questions on a five-item scale. Ten questions with a five-item scale were used to assess the self-concept mode. The role-function mode was assessed using eight questions with a five-item scale, and the interdependence mode was assessed with 6 questions with a five-item scale. Results of the study led the researchers to conclude that RAM-based patient education could improve adaptation in the physiologic and self-concept modes. More research is recommended in this area.

The patient-family-nurse experience in the intensive care unit (ICU) is unique and different for all involved. A qualitative phenomenological study was done to examine patients, their families, and nurses' experiences in the ICU and to explore the meaning of those experiences from the individual's perspective. Cypress (2011) conducted the study with a total of 15 participants. One male and four females between the ages of 25 to 60 years made up the nurse sample. Patient sample was four males and one female between the ages of 22 to 70 years. Family members included one male and four females in the age range of 22 to 70 years. Over a 5-6 month period data were collected through audiotaped interviews. The van Manen's line-by-line approach was used to analyze and code the data. Content analysis revealed five integrated themes that reflected concepts from the RAM. Cypress (2011) reported interdependence as the overarching theme that evolved from the data concerning participants' experiences. The researcher suggested that the results from the data may benefit nursing practice, education, and research. Cypress (2011) suggested that more quantitative and qualitative studies should be done to explore the RAM between the themes that emerged from the study data.

Finally, Gagliardi, Frederickson and Shanley (2002), conducted a qualitative naturalistic case study to understand the experiences of individuals living with multiple sclerosis (MS). The study was based on the concepts of RAM. Data collection was done over a 12-month period on study participants that were selected from the National

Multiple Sclerosis Society using the purposive sampling method. There were 18 participants in the study. The sample consisted of nine females and nine males with age ranges between 27 to 61 years. More than 75% of the sample was White, two were Eastern Europeans, one was African American, and one was Italian American. Participants were diagnosed with MS at ages between 21 and 49 years.

According to Gagliardi et al. (2002), three guided conversations were done in the data collection process. The first in-depth interview format included global questions that were designed to obtain a general perception of each participant's experiences of living with and adapting to MS. The interviews were done in three phases that were either telephonic or in person and was audiotaped. General questions were used to promote participation and to provide an opportunity for the researchers to access participant's feelings and thoughts. Data were transcribed, coded, and separated into themes. Analysis of the data revealed five themes reflecting the RAM concepts of adaption, as well as providing guidance for nursing interventions that would ultimately enhance quality of life for individuals living with MS. Gagliardi, et al. (2002) suggested the need for further studies to expand ways in which the RAM modes of adaptation are interrelated.

Summary of Prevalence of RAM in Research

Evidence from this literature review showed the global and local use of RAM as a theoretical framework for several studies in an effort to determine coping and adaptation. The literature review revealed that the RAM can be used to determine (a) coping and adaptation of Taiwanese families, (b) to determine the application and effectiveness in pregnant women experiencing nausea and vomiting, (c) investigation of adaptation and coping in liver transplant, (d) coping and adaption in army reservists soldier, (e) development of a RAM-based education plan for specific populations, and (f) revelation of positive adaptions using the RAM for patients with multiple sclerosis. Review of the literature also discovered the use of RAM in other military populations but none addressed coping and adaptation in nurses, particularly in veteran army nurses with combat-related PTSD. This gap supports the need for further studies such as this one, which researches the use of RAM pertaining to army registered nurses and specifically to this population of veteran army nurses with combat-related PTSD. A summary of the literature review is presented in Table 2.

Table 2

Matrix of Prevalence of RAM

Author	Year	Focus	Methodology	Conclusions/ Findings
Li & Shyu	2007	Coping process of Taiwanese families.	Qualitative Grounded Theory	Maintaining harmony was a core concept in the coping measures of the Taiwanese families.
Isbir & Mete	2013	Effectiveness of RAM in describing experiences of pregnant women with nausea and vomiting.	Qualitative Exploratory	Stimuli triggering nausea and vomiting in pregnant women varied and responses to the stimuli were different.
Ordin, Karayurt, & Wellard	2013	Using RAM to investigate adaptation in post liver transplant individuals.	Qualitative Descriptive	Individuals demonstrated both effective and ineffective adaptation behaviors.
Looper	2012	Adaptation and Coping using RAM in the	Qualitative Secondary Analysis	Support for the concepts of RAM and the CAPS.

		study of army reservists.		
Afrasiabifar, Karimi,& Hassani	2013	RAM-based patient education.	Quantitative Semi-experimental	Supported a RAM-based patient education for hemodialysis patients.
Cypress	2011	Patients, families, nurses in the ICU during critical illness and the concepts of RAM.	Qualitative Phenomenology	Interdependence was the overarching theme in patients efforts to cope and adapt.
Gagliardi, Frederickson & Shanley	2002	Adaptation of patients with MS using the RAM concepts.	Qualitative Case study	Themes were developed from the data that suggested the need for use of RAM as a teaching method in patients with MS..
Total Number of Research Studies	8			

Prevalence of PTSD in the Military Community

PTSD is not specific to the military, and data to determine the prevalence are scarce. However, approximately 7-8% of America's population will develop PTSD at some time in their lives, and in any given year about 8 million adults receive a diagnosis of PTSD (Gradus, 2015). To determine the prevalence of PTSD in the military community, the National Vietnam Veterans Readjustment Study (NVVRS) was done. The study comprised of 3,016 American Veterans who were interviewed over a two-year period. Results of the study revealed a 30.9% lifetime prevalence of PTSD among male veterans, and 26.9% for women (Kulka et al., 1990).

To estimate PTSD prevalence in Gulf War Veterans, Kang, Natelson, Mahan, Lee, and Murphy (2003) conducted a quantitative experimental study with a population-based sample of 15,000 Gulf War Veterans. The PTSD checklist (PCL-9) was used to assess PTSD in the participants. Individuals with scores of 50 or higher on the PTSD Checklist met the criteria for PTSD. Results revealed a 12.1% prevalence of PTSD in Gulf War Veterans, and a 10.1% in the total Gulf War Veteran population. The 2008 epidemiology study conducted by RAND Corporation, Center for Military Health Policy Research was to examine the prevalence of PTSD among Operation Enduring Freedom and Operation Iraqi Freedom (Iraq and Afghanistan) service members. A population-based sample of 1,938 participants were assessed using the PCL-9 Checklist. The prevalence of PTSD was 13.8% (Tanielian & Jaycox, 2008). However, as previously stated, as of September 2014, there are approximately 2.7 million American Veterans of the Iraq and Afghanistan conflicts, and approximately 20% have PTSD and/or comorbid depression (Department of Veterans Affairs, 2015)

PTSD and Other Factors

In the United States, PTSD is categorized as one of the most common psychological disorders affecting individuals. The illness is seen in survivors of traumatic events such as motor vehicle accidents (MVAs), wars, physical and sexual abuse and others. Despite extensive work on PTSD, more research is needed in areas of comorbidity and PTSD (Meffert et al., 2008).

Other Traumas

Trauma can also result from high-stress professions, such as in nursing, emergency services, law enforcement, and the military. Similar to the dangers in a combat environment, law enforcement officers are exposed to significantly high amounts of stress and traumatic events. For example, law enforcement officers are exposed to the deaths of peers and others; additionally, these officers are sometimes required to engage in battle, knowing that they might lose their own lives. Regehr and Bober (2005) posited that although research indicates that individuals who are exposed to trauma suffer from traumatic symptoms, it is unclear whether these symptoms affect the individuals' performance and decision-making capabilities.

A quantitative quasi-experimental study was done by LeBlanc, Regehr, Jelley, and Barath (2007) in which they examined how exposure to trauma and diagnosis of PTSD affected the job performance of police officers. The study sample consisted of 84 police recruits from the basic constable training program and 14 different police services at the Ontario Police College in Canada. At the time of the study, the participants had completed approximately three weeks of a 60-day program. Of the 84 participants, 71.4% were men, 45.8% were single, 36.9% were married, and 16.7% lived with a partner. The mean age was 30.31. Twenty percent of the participants had worked in high-stress jobs, including in fire department, medical, and military positions.

Pre and post-tests were administered. The Critical Incident History Questionnaire (CIHQ) was used to measure participants' prior exposure to critical incidents, and the Impact of Events Scale-Revised (IES-R) was used to measure the existing level of traumatic stress symptoms. Based on the results, the researchers rejected the belief that police recruits with PTSD possess cognitive deficits that affect judgment and communication. However, the authors acknowledged that the simulated stressful events did not expose the recruits to actual threats. Individuals with PTSD or previous exposure to trauma may experience impaired performance when faced with an actual threat (LeBlanc et al., 2007). The authors suggested that more research is necessary to completely understand how PTSD and exposure to trauma affects individuals' performance.

Military sexual trauma (MST) has also been linked to PTSD, depression, anxiety disorders and substance abuse. Victims of MST were nine times more likely to develop PTSD (Conard, Young, Hogan, & Armstrong, 2014). A quantitative retrospective cross-sectional study conducted by Kelly, Skelton, Patel, & Bradley (2011) was done with female veterans who experienced MST to examine the connection between various traumas and PTSD. The sample consisted of 135 female veterans who had care at a VA facility from August 2006 to June 2008. The mean age of participants was 40.3. Study sample included 71.9% African Americans with a combined 17.1% of White, non-Hispanic women. Participants' demographics also revealed that 26.6% of the sample had never been married (Kelly et al., 2011).

Data collection was done through a veteran administration self-report questionnaire that the women completed at their intake interviews, and the trauma histories documented by clinicians at the time of the intake interviews. The data was obtained from a VA database and participants identifying information was removed. Analysis of data was done with PASW 18.0 statistical software. The data revealed 83.1% of participants had experienced MST. When one or more lifetime trauma was added to the MST the result was 95.4%. The most common non-military adult trauma among participants was sexual abuse (77%). Previous abusive relationships accounted for 52.7% of the non-military trauma, while 54.8% reported physical abuse as an adult, and 48.9% reported persistent emotional abuse. Participants who reported physical, sexual, and emotional trauma amounted to 36.7%. The mean score for PTSD symptom severity in participants was 65.15 which was clinically significant (Kelly et al., 2011).

The study findings were indicative of a significant relationship between various traumas and PTSD. Clinical implication of the study is the need to thoroughly assess for non-military trauma in women with PTSD. Future research include the assessment of specific characteristics of MST and their connection to subsequent mental outcomes, as well as determining the correlation between length of service among MST survivors and their ability to function mentally, physically and socially. Study limitations include the inability to generalize the results to a larger sample, the small sample size, and the high percentage of African American participants (Kelly et al., 2011).

With the aim of examining an association between resilience, trauma, PTSD, and posttraumatic growth (PG) Bensimon (2012) did a quantitative cross-sectional study. The study was done in Israel with 493 participants of which 333 were women. The average age of participants was 24.7. Four hypotheses were developed based on the literature on the relationship between trauma, resilience, PTSD, and PG (Bensimon, 2012). Study measures included the Trauma History Questionnaire, the DSM PTSD Inventory, the Connor-Davidson Resilience Scale, and the Posttraumatic Growth Inventory. Results of the study indicated 91.6% of participants had over one exposure to trauma. A total of 94% were classified as having PTSD, and 78.3% reported growth. Using this information the research concluded that there was a positive association with trauma, PTSD, and PG, which supported hypothesis 1; there was a negative association between resiliency and PTSD, which supported hypothesis 2; a positive relationship existed between PTSD and growth, which supported hypothesis 3, and a positive association existed between resilience and growth, which supported hypothesis 4 (Bensimon, 2012). The convenience sample method limited generalizability of the study, as well as the research design weakened the conclusions. It was suggested that future research should examine the issues longitudinally (Bensimon, 2012).

A study was done examining the relationship between military sexual trauma (MST) and nonmilitary sexual trauma and development of PTSD among female Veterans (Himmelfarb, Yaeger, & Mintz, 2006). Participants were recruited from a VA clinic in Los Angeles, and consisted of 196 female veterans. The women were recruited by viewing a flier listing the services provided to women, and were asked to participate in a study about stress in which they would receive $5.00 in VA canteen coupons. Additionally, an invitation letter was mailed to female veterans in the area soliciting their participation. A cross-sectional design was used in the study. A total of 196 female veterans participated in the study. The sample was diverse with 39.5% White, 39% African Americans, 11.7% Latina, Asian 3.1%, and 2.6% Other. The sample ratio was 43.9% Army veterans, 25% Air Force veterans, 24% Navy veterans, and 6.6% Marine veterans. Mean age was 48 years old. The findings indicated that 72% of participants had previously experienced some kind of sexual trauma, 41% had MST, 19% were assaulted prior to joining the military, and 24% were sexually assaulted after leaving the military. Further, 60% of the MST group, 47% of the pre-military group, and 55% of the post military group had developed PTSD (Himmelfarb et al., 2006). The researchers concluded that because the military population was not compared with a civilian population, they could not conclude that military service increased the risk of sexual assault or increased the risk for PTSD after the assault occurs. Generalizability, the clinical population, and participants' reasons for participating were some of the study's limitations (Himmelfarb et al., 2006).

Preexisting Psychiatric Illnesses

Sandweiss et al. (2011) conducted a prospective longitudinal study involving more than 22,600 soldiers. The objective of the study was to evaluate the association of service members' psychiatric condition before deployment and the severity of injury with postdeployment PTSD. From the number of qualified participants (N = 22,630), 8.1% were positive for PTSD at follow-up, and 0.8% incurred a physical injury that was deployment related. Sandweiss et al. (2011) reported that the probability of screening positive for PTSD symptoms was 2.52 times greater in participants with baseline mental health disorders and 16.1% greater in those with an increase in their Injury Severity Score. Based on the data confidence level, statistic, and margin of error, there was a 95% confidence interval associated with the data from each group. Results of the study indicated that soldiers with preexisting mental illness are more likely to suffer from PTSD upon returning from combat. Soldiers with depression, anxiety disorders, and other psychiatric illness prior to being deployed are more than twice as likely to develop PTSD compared to soldiers who did not have psychiatric illnesses before being deployed. Among the participants, approximately 3% had a psychiatric diagnosis before deployment. After deployment, approximately 8% exhibited symptoms of PTSD (Sandweiss et al., 2011).

In a quantitative longitudinal study conducted by Crain, Larson, Highfill-McRoy and Schmied (2011) it was discovered that Marines who had a preexisting mental illness were more likely to develop PTSD than those without. The goal of the study was to investigate service members who deployed to combat with a preexisting mental disorder. Study sample consisted of 63,890 medical records of Marines who deployed during 2002-2008, and who had a 6-month postdeployment check-up prior to January 2009. The records were divided into two groups of Marines with preexisting mental health conditions (3,258) and those without a psychiatric illness prior to deployment (60,632) (Crain, et al., 2011). Participants' demographic records revealed the percentage of males without a psychiatric disorder prior to deployment was 96.6%, as opposed to 92.8% of their counterparts. Females were 3.4% and 7.2% with total participants' age of < 21 and ≥ 21 respectively. Race or ethnicity of the non-preexisting group was 71.4% White, 7.5% Black, 15.9% Hispanic, and 5.2% Other/Mixed. Race and ethnicity in the preexisting group was 75.5% White, 6.2% Black, 12.4% Hispanic, and 4.9% of other or mixed race. Results of the study supported an increased risk for PTSD in Marines who deployed with a preexisting psychiatric illness. Whereas Marines in the preexisting group were 3.6 times more likely than their cohorts to develop post mental health illness to include PTSD. Crain, et al. (2011) suggested that based on the findings, it would make sense to enforce a complete medical and psychiatric screening pre and postdeployment to determine whether combat exposure worsened preexisting conditions, or intensified them in those with additional psychiatric illnesses such as PTSD.

Heart Disease

Researchers have not identified a direct link between PTSD and coronary artery disease, but have found that U. S. veterans with PTSD have a greater risk of developing myocardial infarction (Ahmadi et al., 2010). In a quantitative correlational study, the researchers performed coronary artery calcium scanning on 637 veterans without coronary artery disease to determine if there is a direct link between PTSD and heart disease. The higher the score, the greater likelihood of atherosclerosis. The average score for participants with PTSD was 76.1%, compared to an average of 59% for participants without PTSD. The results validated that there is a link between PTSD and heart disease, as well as an independent predictor of mortality. The researchers posited that the study results is an indication of the importance of integrated physical and mental health care. This approach not only helps reduce the potential negative psychological effects but also lowers the risk of negative physical effects (Ahmadi et al., 2010).

PTSD and early-age heart disease mortality was examined by Boscarino (2008). A quantitative prospective study was done to examine early-age heart disease mortality among Vietnam veterans with no previous heart disease. The baseline study was done in 1985 with a random sample of 4,328 male Vietnam veterans. A follow-up study was done in 2000 that assessed various demographics, behaviors, and coping methods in the prediction of heart disease mortality. One hundred and thirty-four veterans were eliminated from the original 4,328 participants. While gathering data for the study, an assessment of the participants vital status was completed over the period 1985-2000. Ascertainment of vital status was obtained using three databases and the determination of status was done by combining all mortality sources.

In addition to age, race, and veteran status several variables were included in the study. Variables included intelligence, history of other mental disorders, smoking history, and body mass index (Boscarino, 2008). Cox regression was used in the analysis of data to calculate multivariate hazard ratios predicting early-age heart disease mortality. Findings from the study indicated that PTSD was associated with heart disease mortality, younger age, and other variables. There were several limitations of the study including the possibility of over reported cause of death. The author posited that long-term stress injuries, in addition to short-term psychological consequences of war are expected to manifest as clinical diseases (Boscarino, 2008).

Other Health Issues

In a cross-sectional, retrospective study, Kaiser, Spiro, Lee, and Stellman (2012) examined data on the physical and mental health of 975 females who served in the Vietnam War. The original study participants' ages ranged from 50 to 70 and older. Majority of study participants were White, representing 96.6% of the total sample. In terms of years in service, 43.8% of the nurses served 4 years or less, and 35.7% served over 20 years. The study results indicated that PTSD can lead to additional psychological problems, such as depression, social isolation, failure to obtain treatment for PTSD and participating in risky behaviors (Kaiser et al., 2012). The researchers did not identify physical consequences of PTSD because of the study sample. The participants were nurses deployed in support of the war, but they did not experience as many threats to their physical danger as did military personnel who were directly engaged in combat. Sampling males and females who directly engaged in fighting might identify physical issues that are associated with PTSD (Kaiser et al., 2012).

Another study was done by Tural, Onder, and Aker (2012) to determine the predictors of major depressive disorder (MDD) which happens during the progression of PTSD. The researchers re-analyzed data that were extracted from an epidemiological study where 683 survivors were examined after a devastating earthquake. In an effort to decrease the risk of distorting the original data, Tural et al. (2012) used descriptive design

49

to analyze the data obtained from the group with PTSD/MDD and the group that had

PTSD without MDD. Finally, data manipulation and analysis were accomplished with

SPSS. Results of the study indicated that comorbid MDD prevented recovery from

PTSD. Furthermore, the results suggested that a reduction in perceived social support,

more psychological distress, and an increase in severe PTSD were associated with the

comorbidity of MDD and PTSD (Tural et al., 2012).

Pacella, Hruska, and Delahanty (2013) completed a meta-analysis of 62 studies on

the relationship between PTSD and the physical health of individuals, as well as factors

that moderate the relationship. The researchers coded for sample size, gender inclusion,

civilians versus veterans as well as sample recruitment, among other variables. Statistical

analysis of the coded data was done using the Comprehensive Meta-Analysis software

program. Results indicated that in comparison to individuals without PTSD, individuals

with PTSD are more likely to experience general health and medical issues, a lower

quality of life, cardiorespiratory problems, gastrointestinal issues, and more frequent and

severe pain. Based on the results, Pacella et al. (2013) asserted that longitudinal research

is needed on the physical health of individuals shortly after experiencing trauma (Pacella

et al., 2013).

Summary of PTSD and Other factors

A review of the literature revealed some correlation between PTSD and other

illnesses or trauma, which includes heart disease, MVAs, anger, stress, and preexisting

psychiatric illnesses. The studies presented were a representation of various people

groups. A review of the literature did not produce findings on PTSD and comorbidities

in nurses, specifically in veteran army nurses with combat-related PTSD. Presentation of studies on comorbidities and PTSD is relevant to this study because it revealed a gap in the literature on PTSD and comorbidities, and how they relate to coping and adaptation in nurses - specifically in veteran army nurses. A summary of the literature review is presented in Table 3. Although not the focus of this study, determination of a correlation between PTSD and comorbidity, and coping and adaptation, might contribute to coping and adaptation in nurses, - specifically veteran army nurses with combat-related PTSD.

Table 3

Matrix of PTSD and Other Factors

Author	Year	Focus	Methodology	Conclusion/Findings
LeBlanc, Regehr, & Barath	2007	PTSD and Job Performance	Quantitative Quasi-experimental Design	No evidence that PTSD affects job performance in police officers.
Sandweiss et al.,	2011	Military members psychiatric condition before and after deployment and PTSD	Prospective Quantitative Longitudinal Design	Soldiers with psychiatric illnesses prior to deployment were more than twice as likely to develop PTSD compared to soldiers with no psychiatric illnesses predeployment.
Ahmadi et al.,	2010	Determination of a direct link between PTSD and heart disease	Quantitative Correlational Design	There was an apparent link between PTSD and heart disease.
Boscarino	2008	Examination of early-age heart disease and PTSD	Prospective Quantitative Descriptive Design	PTSD was associated with heart disease mortality and younger age.
Kaiser, Spiro, Lee, & Stellman	2012	PTSD and war-zone stress in women nurses deployed to Vietnam	Retrospective Quantitative Study Descriptive Design	PTSD could lead to additional psychological and psychosocial problems.
Tural, Onder, & Aker	2012	Effects of major depressive disorder on PTSD recovery	Retrospective Quantitative Study Descriptive Design	Comorbid major depressive disorder prevented recovery from PTSD.

Pacella, Hruska, & Delahanty	2013	Examined associations between physical health and PTSD	Quantitative Meta-analysis	Individuals with PTSD experienced more health problems, lower quality of life, and severe pain among other illnesses.
Kelly, Skelton, Patel, & Bradley	2011	Correlation of lifetime trauma and PTSD	Quantitative Retrospective Cross-sectional	There was significant correlation between lifetime trauma and PTSD.
Bensimon	2012	Association between resilience, trauma, PTSD, and PG	Quantitative Cross-sectional	All four hypotheses were supported by the results of the study.
Crain, Larson, Highfill-McRoy & Schmied	2011	Preexisting mental health illness and development of PTSD and other mental health issues in Marines	Quantitative Longitudinal	Study results supported the development of PTSD and other mental health illness in Marines with preexisting mental health issues.
Himmelfarb, Yaeger & Mintz	2006	Pre and post-military sexual trauma and effects on PTSD.	Quantitative Cross-sectional	No definitive conclusion that MST and pre-military trauma increase the risks of PTSD.
Total number of research studies	11			

Conceptual Overview of Coping and Adaptation

The concepts of coping and adaptation have existed for a long time. Coping is a key concept for theory and research on adaptation and health. In the late 1970s, a significant shift in coping theory and research occurred when the general view of coping as a trait was abandoned and replaced with the opposing idea that coping was a process (Lazarus, 1993). An examination of coping and its consequences as a process revealed that the concept of emotion was a component of coping with stress. By extracting the variable of emotion, Lazarus (1993) supported the concept that coping evolved according to the environment in which the coping occurred. Further research resulted in a shift of the concept from being a reaction to emotion, to the concept of coping existing in an active relationship (Lazarus, 1991, 1999).

Frydenberg (2002) introduced the concept of coping as a multidimensional process involving more than one systemic chain of events continuing throughout a person's life. Therefore, coping is a dynamic collaboration between individuals and their environments (Frydenberg, 2002). Resulting from the revised conceptualization of coping, the consequent expansion of the theory, and inductive and deductive pragmatic approaches, Roy developed the RAM. Roy integrated the adaptive modes of RAM with the middle-range theory of cognitive processing to develop a middle-range theory of coping and adaptation processing (Roy, 2011b).

Coping and Adaptation

Coping and adaptation are critical to the existence and survival of people. Military service members and nurses among other career groups are at significant risk for developing PTSD. In the critical care subspecialty of nursing, nurses are sometimes faced with challenging, critical patients, which puts them at an increased risk of developing problems like PTSD (Mealer, Jones, & Moss, 2012). This increased risk meant that ICU nurses among others, sometime develop ways to effectively cope and adapt so they can remain working in serious environments such the ICU. Mealer et al. (2012) did a qualitative interpretive study to identify strategies used by ICU nurses who demonstrated resiliency to continue working in the stressful ICU environment. The study aim was to develop deterrent treatments to preclude the development of PTSD in ICU nurses.

Stratified purposeful sampling was used to select 27 participants of which 13 were highly resilient and 14 had a diagnosis of PTSD. Participants' demographics revealed 100% (13) female who were highly resilient, and 93% (14) had PTSD. The nurses were representative of five types of ICUs. Data were collected through telephone interviews that were audio-taped and analyzed manually. Results of the study identified significant characteristics of effective resiliency and coping skills used by ICU nurses. Characteristics of resilience included optimism, development of moral beliefs, and finding a resilient role model. Additional findings from the study indicated the benefits of providing a resilience training program for nurses. The researchers concluded that despite the study sample being nurses, the findings may be applicable to other clinicians.

Badour, Blonigen, Boden, Feldner, and Bonn-Miller, (2012) used a sample of 1,073 military veterans to test the bi-directional association between avoidance coping and the severity of PTSD before and after receiving PTSD treatment. Participants in the quantitative longitudinal study were 88.9% males with a mean age of 52.39 years old. The PCL-M instrument was used to measure the severity of participants' symptoms. Three other scales were used to measure avoidance coping. Sample participants were 58.6% White, 17.4% African Americans, and 14.4% Hispanic with the remaining percentages categorized as other. Descriptive analysis of the data yielded results that suggested veterans with chronic PTSD and high avoidance coping prior to seeking treatment were more apt to sustain the severe symptoms of PTSD while in treatment and eventually became resistant to treatment (Badour et al., 2012). The researchers posited that there might have been increased confidence in the results if clinical interviews were done to measure the severity of PTSD symptoms. The retrospective self-report measure of avoidance coping was also a limitation of the study. Future research is suggested to examine reciprocal associations between PTSD symptom severity and event-specific avoidance to determine any emergent themes.

When individuals effectively adjust to environmental changes, they in turn affect their environment which leads to preservation of the human systems (Roy, 2009). Martz, Bodner, and Livneh (2009) did a quantitative retrospective research study to explore how coping altered the impact of PTSD on psychosocial adjustment among Vietnam Veterans. Two hypotheses were the basis for the study: disability was related to poorer psychosocial adaptation and problem-solving coping was positively related and emotion-focused coping was negatively related to psychosocial adaptation. Data from the U.S. National Vietnam Veterans Readjustment Study (NVVRS) were analyzed to examine the research question. Total sample size was 1,536. A moderation model was used for the research based on the view that coping significantly influenced the direction of the associations between the variables. Folkman and Lazarus' Ways of Coping Checklist was used in the original study. The variables in the current study were *psychosocial adaptation, disability (PTSD),* and *coping*. The original scores on those variables were reversed.

Scores for each dimension of coping were reversed so that higher scores would show higher levels of that coping dimension. A 12-item scale developed by the researchers of the NVVRS was used to assess psychosocial adaptation. Participants' scores on this dimension were summed up and scored reversely to indicate better psychosocial adaptation. Responses to the disability variable were also reversely scored to show a greater degree of a service-connected physical disability. Study findings

55

showed that PTSD negatively influenced psychosocial adaptation among participants, but problem-solving coping facilitated adaptation to PTSD when PTSD symptoms were less severe (Martz et al., 2009). Generalizability was limited to Vietnam veterans. Availability of information on the reliability of some variables were limited. These were some limitations of the study. Martz et al. (2009) concluded that the findings may be cause for further research on how other populations with disabilities solve problems.

As seen in the literature, PTSD and trauma do not affect Americans only, nor are they specific to the military. Park, Chang, and You (2015) conducted a quantitative cross-sectional study in Korea to examine if coping flexibility protected Korean adults who were exposed to trauma and if coping flexibility moderated the association between clinical symptoms of PTSD, depression, and traumatic events. The Perceived Ability to Cope with Trauma (PACT), Posttraumatic Stress Diagnostic Scale (PDS-K), and the PHQ-9 were used to assess 510 participants who had a history of traumatic events (Park, Chang, &You, 2015). Social networking was the method used for recruiting participants. The mean age was 29.25 years and most of the sample were women. Among the traumatic events were sexual assaults, furem illness, natural diaster, imprisonment, torture, and combat. Analysis of the data supported the hypothesis that the ability to alternate coping styles is beneficial in preventing psychological distress among those who were exposed to trauma. The second hypothesis was partially supported. Coping flexibility mediated the association between traumatic events and PTSD, but that mediating effect was absent in the association between traumatic events and depressive symptoms. Because the sample was composed of majority females the sample structure was viewed as a limitation that affected the generalizability to other groups. The study

56

design and recruiting methods were also study limitations. Researchers suggested future research using various samples to investigate the outcome of coping flexibility on adversed mental health after a trauma (Park, Chang, &You 2015).

Tiet et al. (2006) examined the relationship between approach coping and positive outcomes, and the reciprocal relationships between coping and PTSD symptoms in individuals with PTSD. Five VA medical centers on the West Coast were used to select a quarter of the study sample based on the last two digits of their personal identification number. The remaining sample was taken from the clinical intake records of those who received treatment at the five VA medical centers. The number of those who were eligible was 605, and 265 of that number completed a baseline survey. There was no reported significant difference in participants gender, race, military status, or length of service. The study employed a quantitative longitudinal method. (Tiet, et al., 2006). Data analysis was done using structural equation model and the AMOS computer software. Results showed that despite chronic PTSD, approach coping was a predictor of scoietal functioning; cognitive avoidance coping predicted increased PTSD symptoms, and PTSD symptoms were predictors of more avoidance and approach coping. Important limitations of the study were the reliability of the measure of family and social functioning despite their asociation with PTSD symptoms. Also, the sample was mostly men who were veterans seeking treatment at the VA. Future research was suggested using better quality measures for family and social functioning. Because the study could not be generalized, it was suggested that the study be replicated using a larger mixed sample.

Finally, Padden, Connors, and Agazio, (2011) did a quantitative descriptive correlational study to examine the relationship between coping and other stressors in female spouses of active duty soldiers. Lazarus and Folkman's theory of stress and coping was used as the theoretical framework. The study sample consisted of 105 female spouses of active duty soldiers who were deployed at the time of the study. Several stress and coping instruments were used to gather pertinent data. Differences in coping strategies were found, especially in participants whose spouses grew up in a military family and those whose spouses had a previous deployment.

Contextual Factors Affecting Coping and Adaptation

People are regularly confronted with minor challenges. Individuals may also face unusual or traumatic stressors such as those experienced in combat. To effectively cope and adapt, humans develop a constantly changing relationship between self and the environment. Various factors might influence effective coping and adaptation; this was demonstrated in a review of the literature discussed in the following subsections, as well as a summary of the contextual factors (Table 4) influencing coping and adaptation.

Gender. Gender is one factor that might impact susceptibility to adverse effects of trauma, as well as how individuals respond to and manage these reactions (Kimerling, Gima, Smith, Street, & Frayne, 2007). A quantitative secondary analysis study was done by Gibbons, Barnett, Hickling, Herbig-Wall, and Watts (2012) to illustrate the role of gender in coping, and health-seeking behaviors of veteran health care providers. The healthcare providers referred to were veterans of OEF and OIF conflicts and were both officers and enlisted service members. The secondary content analysis was based upon the 2005 Survey of Health Related Behaviors of Active Duty Military (HRB) conducted by the Research Triangle International (Gibbons et al., 2012).

Of the 23,440 original surveys conducted by HRB, 16,146 were used for the study. Participants in the original study were from all branches of the military and consisted of 4,652 enlisted females and 13,589 enlisted males. Participants in the officer group consisted of 1,156 females and 4,043 males. Females in the enlisted group were 40.9% White, 42.3% Black, 11.2% Asian, and 5.6% other. Enlisted males were 49.9% White, 24.4% Black, 10.5% Asian, and 15.2% other. Female participants in the officer category were 83.7% White, 3.6% Black, 6.5% Asian, and 6.1% other. Ethnicity of the male participants were 87.1%, 1.9% Black, 7.0% Asian, and 4.0% other. (Gibbons et al., 2012). Results of the study indicated that factors like socioeconomic status and culture impacted gender differences for stress and coping. Differences in gender coping were more noticeable because of deployments. In addition to gender, minority and differences in rank were also reflected in the study results. Gibbons et al., (2012) suggested that healthcare providers may need to be more sensitive to gender differences when assessing coping and mental health-seeking behaviors in individuals.

For the purpose of examining the impact of sex differences in coping strategies in response to trauma. Schmied et al. 2015 conducted a quantitative prospective study. The larger study was done between October 2011 and 2012. The current study used data collected during the Survival Evasion Resistance and Escape (SERE) training where service members trained in an intense, high risk environment. Participants included 156 males and 44 females with a median age of 25.1. Majority of participants were White (66.9%) males and 70.5% females. Participants completed surveys pre, and 24 hours post the mock activity exercise. Demographics, post-traumatic stress symptoms (PTSS), and coping strategies were the variables assessed. Statistical analysis was done using SPS statistical software, version 19.0. Results of the study revealed gender differences as a potential factor in coping. Gender differences were identified in the use of specific coping strategies. Study data suggested the need for modified coping skills training that focus on the unique needs of men and women (Schmied, et al., 2015).

Another study was done by (Bhutto & Imtiaz, 2011) to determine if there were gender differences in coping. The researchers hypothesized there was a significant difference in coping strategies of males and females. The quantitative descriptive study sample was 150 participants in the age range of 18 to 26 years and a mean age of 21.32 years. Seventy-five males and 75 females made up the total sample. Demographic information also included family income, area of residence, and educational status. Based on the results of the study, Bhutto and Imtiaz (2011) concluded that except for one component of avoidance coping, there was no significant gender differences in coping.

Exclusion of the emotion component is the rationale used to conclude that the research hypothesis was partially proven (Bhutto & Imtiaz, 2011). The researchers discussed several recommendations for future studies: (1) the collection of data from socioeconomic strata to determine the impact, (2) conducting separate studies for males and females (3) conducting studies on illiterate participants because the educational status of participants was intermediate and beyond, (4) increased sample size, and (5) use of a constant stress factor (Bhutto & Imtiaz, 2011).

Each conflict that America was involved with had different approaches and therefore different effects and experiences of individuals who fought in those wars. Advances in medicine and technology, and women in combat impacted the outcomes of those wars. Conard and Sauls (2014) did a quantitative systematic review of deployment and PTSD in the female veteran. At the time of the study, 52% of females had been deployed to either to the Gulf, Iraq, or Afghanistan wars in various roles. A systematic review was done on 10 articles accessed from several databases. Various keywords were used in the search that yielded 285 articles that were further reduced based on relevance and inclusion criteria. Of the 285 articles, 36 were relevant. Additional screening of the articles resulted in the 10 articles used for the study. Findings of the study indicated that length and frequency of deployments might be disadvantageous to the health of combat veterans. However, in an effort to properly assess and provide the best care for veterans, there should be a difference in the approach to care between males and females because many veterans used different coping strategies to deal with the challenges of deployments (Conard & Sauls, 2014). The researchers also suggested that more studies with a larger subsamples of females would be necessary to examine the effects of multiple deployments and how combat veterans were coping with PTSD and other mental health issues after deployment (Conard & Sauls, 2014).

Culture. Culture is another factor that influences the coping and adaptation process. For instance, Aldwin (2007) identified four ways in which culture influences coping: (a) culture affects the kinds of stressors that an individual is likely to experience; (b) culture affects how an individual appraises stressors, (c) culture affects the coping strategies an individual chooses, and (d) culture provides various methods for individuals

61

to use to cope with stress. As the discussion on culture and coping continues to expand, Ghafoori, Barragan, Tohidian, and Palinkas, (2012) did a quantitative cross-sectional study on the relationship between race/ethnicity and the severity of PTSD and generalized anxiety disorder (GAD) in an urban community clinic. A total of 170 participants of diverse ethnicity who were exposed to trauma were selected for the study. Participants were over 18 years old, spoke English, and had experienced some type of trauma. Recruitment occurred prior to participants receiving any kind of mental health treatment. Participants received a noncash incentive of $10.00 for their participation.

A 4-item questionnaire measuring coping was administered to participants. Several other instruments were used in the study to include the PTSD Checklist-Civilian version, The GAD among others. Analysis of the data indicated that Black males were exposed to more trauma (77.8%), and Hispanic females were exposed to more trauma (45.7%) in comparison to the other racial/ethnic groups. Study results also indicated there was no significant relationship between racial/ethnic group status and symptom severity (Ghafoori et al., 2012). Study design, lack of information on coping in those who did not report a traumatic event, and the psychometrics were some limitations discussed (Ghafoori et al., 2012).

Culture shapes how an individual responds to coping and adaptation, stress, and resiliency. Roy (2009) posited that culture as a stimuli affects coping and adaptation. Utsey, Bolden, Lanier, and Williams, 2007 examined the effects of culture-specific coping and resiliency in African Americans living in high-risk communities. The quantitative cross-sectional study consisted of 361 African American participants of which 165 were men and 195 were women. Participants' ages ranged from 18 to 69.

The convenience sampling method was used to recruit participants located in an urban area. Survey packets were completed by each participant, and he or she received a compensation of $20.00 for their time. Several instruments were used to gather data. The Structured Equation Model software program was used in the data analysis (Utsey et al., 2007). Results of the study revealed that cultural and traditional factors affect coping in African Americans. Limitations of the study precludes it from generalizability. Future research in risk and resilience was suggested.

To examine the relationship between culture and coping, Westhius, Fafara, and Ouellette (2006) conducted a quantitative exploratory study to determine if ethnicity affects coping in military spouses. Study data was taken from the 4,464 individuals of a Survey of Army Families done in 2001. Questionnaires were mailed to a stratified comparative sample of 20,000 civilian spouses of active army soldiers worldwide. Responses from the survey totaled 6,759 spouses who returned completed surveys (Westhuis et al., 2006). Of the sample, 9.5% were African American, and 8.7% were Hispanic or of other races. The sample majority was females (96.3%) with a mean age of 34.5 years. A 5-step process was used to analyze the data. Results from the study indicated a statistical significance between ethnicity and coping. Based on these results, it was recommended that ethnicity should be considered when developing support programs for military spouses. The study sample consisted of civilian spouses only. Limitations of the study included study design, preexisting sample, and generalizability (Westhuis et al., 2006).

Concept of self. Trauma of any type can affect individuals' concept of self. It causes lower self-esteem and lower self-image (Slaninova & Stainerova, 2015). In this study, self-esteem was reported by 50% of participants who apparently felt like a diagnosis of PTSD made them less of a person. To determine the impact of trauma on the self-concept of undergraduates, Slaninova and Stainerova (2015) did a qualitative study using a narrative reconstructive design. Study sample was four females and one male in their late adolescent and early adulthood who were first or second year undergraduate students. During their psychotherapy, 10 in-depth interviews were collected from students who experienced some type of trauma in their childhood, late adolescent or early adulthood. Five interviews were used for the study. The topics of focus included students' values and beliefs, reflection and perspective, as well as their self-images and the images of others (Slaninova & Stainerova, 2015). Results from the data analysis revealed that trauma significantly impacted the self-concept of an individual, which resulted in lower self-image, and self-esteem. Also, in some individuals, trauma contributed to anxiety and depressive symptoms. Slaninova and Stainerova (2015) also concluded the results showed no differences between acute or chronic trauma or between physical and psychological trauma. For future research there was recommendation to conduct more studies using a more detailed process (Slaninova & Stainerova, 2015).

The purpose of a quantitative descriptive study conducted by Thompson and Waltz (2008) was to explore the relationship between the severity of post-traumatic stress symptoms and individuals' low compassion for self and kindness, more self-judgement, and a lower ability to recall painful memories without reliving them. The study sample consisted of 79 males and 131 females who were introductory psychology students. Participant's mean age was 19. The instruments used for the study were the Posttraumatic Stress Diagnostic Scale and the Self-Compassion Scale, both of which were self-report measures. The most common traumas reported were accidents, deaths, and sexual assaults (Thompson & Waltz,2008). Study results showed that the severity of avoidance symptoms was most significant in relation with self-compassion. The researchers discussed the use of experiential avoidance (behaviors that diminish the conflict with painful thoughts, emotions, and sensations) as one way to understand the relationship between the severity of avoidance symptom and lower-self-compassion. Further, that recall of the trauma elicits fear in an individual resulting in avoidance behaviors and judgmental responses toward self. Individuals with high self-compassion are less likely to feel fearful and more likely to undergo the normal course of exposure to trauma-related stimuli. Limitations discussed were self-report of trauma and the uncertainty of whether trauma exposure and PTSD symptoms contributed to lower self-compassion or if low self-compassion made individuals more vulnerable to develop PTSD. Thompson and Waltz (2008) suggested that despite the study results, it might be useful to integrate self-compassion into trauma treatment, specifically to address self-criticism and reflection because self-criticism and rumination are experiences associated with trauma and PTSD.

Traumatic brain injuries (TBI) occurring from blasts during the Iraq and Afghanistan wars have increased significantly. More often, individuals with TBI also suffers with PTSD. Therefore, it is important that clinicians understand that individuals need treatment of both conditions (Warden, 2006). Ponsford, Kelly, and Couchman

(2014) conducted a quantitative comparative study to examine global self-concept, specific self-concept dimensions, self-esteem, and anxiety levels and depression symptoms between two sample groups. Study sample consisted of 41 participants who had brain injury and 41 who did not. The brain injury group was made up of 70% male, and all study participants were over 18 years old and had enough perceptive skills to complete the study measures. The group had a mean age of 39.36 years old. The participants were recruited from a rehabilitation center in the community. Participants in the control group were volunteers from various sources in the community and comprised of 70.7% males with a mean age of 38.70.

Several instruments were used to measure the study variables. Both groups were compared in global self-concept and self-esteem; dimensions of self-concept, mood, and inter-relationships of self-concept, self-esteem, and mood. Data analysis produced results that were indicative of significant lower self-concept and lower self-esteem among the TBI group versus the control group (Ponsford et al., 2014). Participants in the TBI group rated themselves as socially isolated from peers and avoided taking social risks. They also reported being alienated from their family and poor marital relationships. Study limitations were sample size and inability to generalize. Future suggestions for research included the determination of whether time and adjustment to injury would result in changes in self-concept, self-esteem and/or mood (Ponsford et al., 2014).

Religion/spirituality. Religion/spirituality is seen in the everyday lives of people. For some, it provides hope and a way of coping. A quantitative cross-sectional study was done with 164 participants who were cancer patients. Baljani, Khashabi, Amanpour, and Azimi, (2011) conducted the study using convenience sampling to select participants with the intent to determine what relationship, if any, exists between spirituality, religion, and hope. A four-part questionnaire was used for data collection. Results indicated that spiritual well-being and religion affected hope in the cancer patients. The researchers suggested the results could help nurses to understand the importance of spiritual well-being and religion to increase hope in patients (Baljani et al., 2011).

To address the issue of prayer and its relationship to Post-traumatic growth (PTG), Harris et al. (2010) did a quantitative cross-sectional study to identify what specific prayer functions were related to PTG. Two hypotheses were used to guide the study, (1) it may be difficult for survivors of interpersonal trauma to use prayer as a coping strategy, which may result in the perception of less PTG, and (2) was there a weaker relationship between prayer-coping functions and PTG in survivors of interpersonal trauma than for non-interpersonal trauma survivors. Random sampling was used to recruit 327 trauma survivors as study participants. The sample consisted of 228 females, 95 males, and 1 transgendered participant, all from various denominations with an average age of 55 years old. Participants received an incentive of $10.00. Several instruments were used for data collection. Harris et al. (2010) concluded that, based on the study results, both hypotheses were partially supported. It was suggested that longitudinal studies may address the issue more appropriately, as well as using a larger sample.

Religious practices facilitate strong social support from fellow believers that may motivate individuals with PTSD to seek mental health services. Several factors can weaken religious faith and practices. When individuals are in combat situations, killing and being unable to stop the death of others significantly increases the likelihood of feeling guilt and developing PTSD. Furthermore, the severity of combat exposure is directly linked with the severity of PTSD. A combination of these elements weakens an individual's religious faith (Fontana & Rosenheck, 2004). A quantitative correlation study employing structural equation modeling was conducted by Fontana and Rosencheck (2004). The purpose of the study was to observe a model of the correlations between the traumatic exposure of veterans, their experience with PTSD, guilt, change in religious faith, and their continuous use of mental health services. The study sample consisted of more than 1,384 veterans who provided data for evaluation of the VA's inpatient and outpatient PTSD programs. The investigators collected data from 1989 to 1994 from participants with consecutive admissions to a total of 16 PTSD programs provided by the VA. Of the number of participants (N = 1,385), 94% had a diagnosis of PTSD and the remaining 6% had other mental illnesses. Findings from the study indicated that veterans seek out mental health services because they were apparently driven by guilt and a decline in religious faith rather than by their PTSD symptoms or a lack in their social contact. Additionally, study results indicated that as individuals experienced a decline in religious faith, they lost a sense of belonging and therefore seek out mental health services to fulfill that essential need (Fontana & Rosencheck, 2004).

There are many challenges that affect the lives of urban families. To identify and investigate emotional coping strategies, satisfaction with life, and religion and spirituality among urban families, Doolittle, Courtney, and Jasien, (2015) conducted a quantitative cross-sectional study. The convenience sampling method was used to select families consisting of 127 individuals from various ethnic groups. Parents who brought their children to the local clinic were administered a written English-language questionnaire for demographic data collection. Three additional instruments were used in the study. JMP software was used for statistical analyses. Results revealed several findings including poverty among the families, more than half the children had chronic illnesses and financial challenges among others. Data from the study revealed that when those mentioned variables are added together with spirituality and interpersonal relationships, individuals survive and thrive (Doolittle et al., 2015). The clinical implications for healthcare providers were that, urban individuals had significant emotional and spiritual coping strategies despite poverty and (Doolittle et al., 2015).

Psychological distress and poor mental health exists among individuals who experienced trauma. Freh, Dallos, and Chung, (2012) conducted a qualitative phenomenological study to explore how people made sense of their experiences, and identified coping strategies in the aftermath of a bombing. Nine adults (male = 4, female = 5) who experienced a bomb attack were recruited for the study. Semi-structured interviews were conducted and transcribed verbatim. Interpretative phenomenological analysis was used to analyzed the data. Results indicated that among many other effects, exposure to a bomb attack had a significant effect on core beliefs. Also, that individuals demonstrated a variety of coping strategies, which included prayer, religion, and the use of religious objects.

Substance abuse. Miller, Kaloupek, Dillon, and Keane (2004) did a quantitative longitudinal study replicating and extending prior findings of the effects of personality on internalizing and externalizing subtypes of PTSD. Internalizers are those who believe that setting goals and working hard to achieve will bring results. Internalizers take responsibility when things go wrong and modify or adjust to achieve better results next time. Externalizers believe that circumstances beyond their control can stop their goals. They often do not take responsibility for their actions because nothing is their fault.

Study participants were male military veterans who served in Vietnam during a certain time frame. The subsample of 736 males were taken from the previous study. The sample was partitioned into externalizing and internalizing groups. Data analysis showed that externalizers demonstrated the highest rates of alcohol-related and antisocial personality disorders and were most likely to screen positive for alcohol on a urine toxicology screen. Internalizers had the highest rates of panic and major depressive disorder and showed the most severe forms of PTSD. Future research on the topic was suggested, using other variables. Limitations were the study design and sample which consisted of entirely male.

The use of alcohol as a coping measure is considered maladaptive behavior. Adams, Boscarino, and Galea, (2006) conducted a quantitative retrospective study of 1,681 participants to examine the relationship between alcohol use and mental health status. The study was done within the context of the 9/11 attacks. Participants ages ranged from 18-65 years old. The racial breakdown was: 43% White, 26% African American, 24.1% Latino, and 7% other. The researchers reported binge drinking or alcohol dependence was related to worse mental health. An unexpected finding was that increased alcohol use was associated with better physical health. Adams et al. (2006) posited that increased alcohol use that was not unhealthy use seemed to lower stress and the negative physical consequences on physical health. Further discussion indicated that individuals may use alcohol to dull the symptoms of PTSD such as hyperarousal, and flashbacks (Adams et al., 2006).

Veenstra et al. (2007) concluded that participants who demonstrated a higher use of emotional coping also demonstrated increased alcohol use. The purpose of this quantitative longitudinal study was to examine the relationship between stressful life-events and alcohol use. The quantitative longitudinal study used data from 1608 males and 1645 that were randomly drawn from a previous study of 16,210. The mean age of participants was 45-70 years old. Several variables were used including alcohol use, coping styles, as well social support. Though the results indicated higher use of emotional coping resulted in higher alcohol use, a lower level of alcohol use was found in individuals who used cognitive coping or who had more social contacts (Veenstra et al., 2007).

According to Pietrzak, Goldstein, Southwick, and Grant (2011) the National Epidemiologic Survey on Alcohol and Related Conditions (NESARC) was the largest epidemiology survey ever conducted, surveying over 34,000 individuals. Data from The NESARC study was used to examine lifetime psychiatric comorbidity of PTSD and partial PTSD. Results of the quantitative retrospective study indicated that among other findings, PTSD and partial PTSD were associated with higher lifetime rates of substance abuse disorders (Pietrzak et al., 2011).

In another study, data from 1,402 males from the Norwegian military were assessed to determine the impact of an individual's resilience resource to stress-related problem drinking in a military population (Bartone, Hystad, Eid, & Brevik 2012). The sample data was obtained from the National Defense Health Survey (NDHS) administered by the Norwegian Armed Forces Health Registry. Participants age ranged from 29 to over 50 years old. Data analysis revealed that resiliency and high avoidance coping were significant predictors of alcohol abuse, and the risks were higher in participants with more recent and harsher deployments. A quantitative retrospective approach was used. An implication of the findings was the possible use of resiliency scores to help identify military personnel at risk for alcohol problems. Currently, the military uses direct measures in alcohol screening, which were insufficient to determine alcohol use among military troops (Bartone et al., 2012).

Family and social relationships. Since the conflicts in Iraq and Afghanistan, the issue of PTSD and the effects on service members and families has gained momentum locally and internationally (Jones, 2011). In an effort to determine how coping, resilience, and social support mediates the relationship between PTSD and social functioning, Tsai, Harpaz-Rotem, Pietrzak, and Southwick (2012) conducted a quantitative cross-sectional study with 164 veterans who had returned from Iraq or Afghanistan. The researchers hypothesized that veterans with PTSD would score lower on measures of relationship and life satisfaction, family cohesion and adaptability, and social functioning than veterans without PTSD. Participants were recruited from the VA mental health and primary care facilities in Connecticut. Several instruments including the PCL-M were used to elicit data. Participants who had PTSD were compared to other veterans recruited from the same treatment facilities with equal demographics, as well as their scores on each study measure (Tsai et al., 2012). Analysis of the data revealed that veterans who screened positive for PTSD reported significantly lower satisfaction with partners, less family cohesion, poorer social functioning, and lower life satisfaction scores. In terms of socio-demographics, and service duty, there were no significant differences between the two groups. Study design, sample size, and the method of self-report to gather data were discussed as limitations. Suggested future research involved the use of diagnostic measures supported by data obtained from family members and close friends (Tsai et al., 2012).

PTSD not only affect the veterans themselves, but it also affected families and social relationships. According to Ray and Vanstone (2009), members of the family unit also suffer from the impact of PTSD. Also, the symptoms of PTSD contributed to the difficulty of maintaining strong family relationships, which complicated the social support and made it more difficult to minimize the impact and severity of PTSD symptoms. Ray and Vanstone (2009) conducted an interpretive phenomenological inquiry to examine how PTSD impacted the veteran's family relationships and how those relationships impacted the veteran's healing from the trauma. A purposive sample of 10 who met the inclusion criteria were selected to participate in the study. The sample included 6 enlisted male soldiers, 2 male Chaplains, 1 male medical assistant and 1 female nurse. Data were collected through tape-recorded in-depth interviews with the 10 participants who were all over 18 years old. Themes emerging from the data were the negative impact of emotional numbing and avoidance, anger on familial relationships, and the struggle to heal from trauma in the presence of emotional withdrawal from family support. Future research recommendations were to do a more in-depth study on the same topics, but to include emotional numbing and anger, and inclusion of friends and family in the treatment process focusing on helping the veteran improve inter-personal skills (Ray & Vanstone, 2009).

In another study done by Meis, Erbes, Polusny, and Compton (2010), the aim was to (a) examine how negative emotionality and comorbid alcohol use contributed to elevated postdeployment PTSD symptoms and relationship problems among OIF soldiers. A quantitative longitudinal approach was used. The sample consisted of 308 National Guard soldiers with recent deployments to Iraq, and who were drawn from a previous study of National Guard soldiers. Participants were surveyed 1 month predeployment and 2-3 months postdeployment using postcard reminders, repeated mailings, and a $50 incentive. There were 277 male and 31 female participants that were primarily White, with an average of 31 years old. Educational and relationship statuses varied. To obtain data, several measures were used that included the PTSD checklist and the Marriage/Intimate Relationship Satisfaction Scale (Meis et al., 2010). Data analysis revealed that soldiers with negative emotionality had an increased risk for severe PTSD symptoms that contributed to lesser quality intimate relationships. There was no evidence that problematic alcohol use impacted PTSD symptoms or the quality of relationships. According to Meis et al, (2010) surprisingly, based on the data, there was no correlation between problematic drinking and increased PTSD symptoms. It was suggested that future studies should be done to assess the functionality of pre and postdeployments relationships. It was also suggested that because of the small sample of female participants, additional research should be done to study the effect of gender on

74

these results. Study findings may not generalized to other military groups such as

enlisted Army soldiers or ethnically diverse samples (Meis et al., 2010).

Table 4

Contextual Factors Affecting Coping

Author	Year	Focus	Methodology	Conclusion/Findings
Gibbons, Barnett, Hickling, Herbig-Wall & Watts	2012	Gender in coping	Quantitative Secondary Analysis	Various factors impacted gender differences for stress and coping.
Schmied et al.,	2015	Gender differences In coping strategies	Quantitative Prospective	Gender differences impacted coping strategies.
Bhutto, & Imtiaz	2011	Gender differences in coping	Quantitative Descriptive	There were no significant differences between gender coping.
Ghafoori, Barragan, Tohidian, & Palinkas,	2012	Relationship between race/ethnicity and PTSD symptoms severity	Quantitative Cross-Sectional	No significant relationship between racial/ethnic group status and symptom severity.
Utsey, Bolden, Lanier, & Williams,	2007	Role of culture-specific coping and its effect	Quantitative Cross-Sectional	Culture affected coping.
Baljani, Khashabi, Amanpour, & Azimi	2011	Concept of culture, religion, and spirituality in cancer patients	Quantitative Cross-Sectional	Spiritual well-being and religion affected hope in cancer patients.
Harris et al.,	2010	Prayer and the relationship to post-traumatic growth	Quantitative Cross-Sectional	Both hypotheses were partially supported.
Doolittle, Courtney, & Jasien	2015	Satisfaction with life, coping, and spirituality among urban families	Quantitative Cross-Sectional	Psychosocial and financial status affected coping.
Mealer, Jones, & Moss	2012	Resiliency and PTSD in ICU nurses	Qualitative Interpretive	ICU nurses possessed significant resiliency and coping skills.
Fontana & Rosencheck	2004	Relationship between religion and seeking mental health services	Quantitative Correlation	When individuals experienced a decline in religious faith, they lose a sense of belonging.
Badour, Blonigen,	2012	Relationship between	Quantitative Longitudinal	Pre-treatment avoidance coping affected PTSD

Boden, Feldner & Bonn-Miller		avoidance coping and PTSD severity during and after PTSD treatment		severity during treatment while PTSD severity increased avoidance coping after treatment.
Martz, Bodner & Livneh	2009	Problem-solving coping effects on Disability and psychosocial adaptation	Quantitative Retrospective	PTSD did not influence psychosocial adaptation.
Slaninova, & Stainerova	2015	Trauma and self-concept	Qualitative Narrative Reconstructive	Trauma experiences could result in low self-esteem and a low concept of self.
Thompson & Waltz	2008	Relationship between trauma exposure and PTSD and self-compassion and kindness	Quantitative Descriptive	Uncertainty of whether trauma exposure and PTSD symptoms contributed to lower self-compassion or if low self-compassion made individuals more vulnerable to develop PTSD.
Ponsford, Kelly & Couchman	2014	Examination of global self-concept between one group with trauma and one group with no trauma	Quantitative Comparative	Significant lower self-concept and lower self-esteem among the TBI group versus the control group.
Park, Chang, & You	2015	Flexibility coping in adults with PTSD and other traumas	Quantitative Cross-sectional	Coping flexibility mediated the association between traumatic events and PTSD.
Tiet et al.,	2006	Approach coping and the effects on PTSD symptoms and social functioning	Quantitative Longitudinal	Approach coping positively affected family and social functioning. PTSD symptoms were predictors of more avoidance and approach coping.
Conard & Sauls	2014	Deployment and PTSD in female veterans	Quantitative Systematic Review	Females were at higher risk for depression and higher exposure to other stressors of combat.
Westhius, Faara & Oullette	2006	Effect of ethnicity on coping of military spouses	Quantitative Exploratory	Ethnicity affected coping and support groups for military

				spouses should consider this factor.
Padden, Connors, & Agazio	2011	Culture and the relationship between stress, coping and general well-being of military spouses.	Quantitative Correlational	Differences in coping strategies were found in military spouses.
Miller, Kaloupek, Dillon, & Keane	2004	How personality and resulting behaviors affect the ability to cope.	Quantitative Longitudinal	Veterans who exhibited high alienation and aggression had a history of substance abuse.
Veenstra, Lemmens, Friesema, Tan, Garretsen, Knottnerus, & Zwietering	2007	Coping styles and alcohol use	Quantitative Longitudinal	Higher use of emotion coping resulted in higher alcohol use.
Pietrzak, Goldstein, Southwick, & Grant	2011	Prevalence of psychiatric comorbidity of PTSD and partial PTSD	Quantitative Retrospective	PTSD and partial PTSD were associated with higher rates of substance abuse.
Adams, Boscarino, & Galea	2006	To examine the relationship between alcohol and mental health status	Quantitative Retrospective	Increased alcohol use resulted in worse mental health.
Freh, Dallos, & Chung	2012	PTSD and coping strategies in individuals who experienced a bomb attack.	Qualitative Phenomenological	Various strategies were used to cope with traumatic events.
Bartone, Hystad, Eid, & Brevik	2012	Individuals resiliency resources and coping styles as factors for alcohol abuse	Quantitative Retrospective	Resiliency and high avoidance coping were significant predictors of alcohol abuse.
Tsai, Harpaz-Rotem, Pietrzak, & Southwick	2012	Coping, resilience, social support, social functioning and PTSD	Quantitative Cross-sectional	Veterans with PTSD reported significantly lower satisfaction with partners, less family cohesion, poorer social functioning, and lower life satisfaction scores.

Ray & Vanstone	2009	The impact of PTSD on family relationship	Qualitative Interpretative Phenomenological	Emotional numbing and anger had a negative impact on familial relationships, and emotional withdrawal from family support creates a struggle with healing from trauma.
Meis, Erbes, Polusny, & Compton,	2010	The role of PTSD symptoms, and alcohol in intimate relationships.	Quantitative Longitudinal	Severe PTSD symptoms impacted relationship, but there was no correlation between problematic drinking and increased PTSD symptoms.
Total Number of Research Studies	29			

This section of the literature review uncovered specific literature relative to the factors that affects coping and adaptation in different populations. This finding is significant because coping and adaptation differs for individuals, and several factors affect the process of coping. The section also concluded the previous sections. The literature presented corresponded with the different strategies that individuals used to cope and adapt with PTSD and other traumatic events. However, a review of the literature did not reveal any studies that delineated coping and adaptation in veteran army nurses with combat-related PTSD. One study revealed resilience and PTSD in a population of civilian critical care nurses. A qualitative research case study focusing on how veteran army nurses cope and adapt with combat-related PTSD would contribute to the existing literature on coping and adaptation. Also, this study would add depth to the topic as it relates to the specific sub-group of veteran army nurses with combat-related PTSD.

State of Evidence

PTSD is one of the most common psychological disorders in the United States and can be the result of various traumatic experiences, including vehicular accidents, child abuse, rape, and combat (Kessler et al., 1995). Sometimes one traumatic event is enough to cause PTSD, but in other cases the condition results when a traumatic event is repeated, such as when in combat and when bullied (Idsoe, Dyregrov, & Idsoe, 2012; McDonald, Danielson, Resnick, Saunders, & Kilpatrick, 2010).

From the findings of this literature review it is plausible to conclude that while studies have been conducted on PTSD and coping, there were none specific to veteran army nurses coping with combat-related PTSD. Also, there appears to be a sparseness of studies relating to coping and adaptation among nurses in general. Conard and Sauls (2014) suggested that more studies would be necessary to examine the effects of multiple deployments, as well as studies using larger subsamples of females, and how combat veterans are coping with PTSD and other mental health issues after deployment. Researchers had not previously explored how RAM applied specifically to veteran army nurses with combat-related PTSD. Data from this study revealed how veteran army nurses cope and adapt with PTSD within the context of the four modes of RAM.

Nayback (2009) highlighted the need to examine RAM in relation to PTSD among vulnerable populations, such as nursing caregivers. Results of this study might contribute to the knowledge in this area of study. There was also a gap in the literature regarding how combat-related PTSD affected the job performance of veteran army nurses. Culture is not limited to ethnicity or race; culture exists in any group or organization, such as the military. The military cultural framework in which soldiers immerse themselves includes unique systems, languages, and practices. This culture includes a focus on self-restraint, unity, and high morale (Nayback, 2009), all of which can influence how soldiers cope and adapt to the stressors experienced in combative environments.

Summary

Chapter two contained a literature review that demonstrated coping and adaptation in different populations and various factors. A review of the literature did not reveal coping and adaptation specifically among veteran army nurses with combat-related PTSD. The area of coping and adaptation in nurses and specifically veteran army nurses with combat-related PTSD required research to fill the gap. Review of the literature began with an overview of PTSD because of its significance in demonstrating the broad range of the effects of this illness in the military population as well as the general population. The history was described and supported within the literature. Comorbidities of PTSD were also found within the literature. The comorbidities include motor vehicle accidents, trauma exposure, preexisting psychiatric illnesses, heart disease, and other health issues which have been found to affect PTSD differently. Then, research involving the RAM was examined. The literature review disclosed current literature regarding the global use of RAM in nursing research. Research was needed specifically regarding the use of RAM and coping and adaption among veteran army nurses with combat-related PTSD. Next, the contextual factors affecting coping and adaptation were discussed within the context of existing literature.

A qualitative research methodology was employed to uncover coping and adaptation in veteran army nurses with combat-related PTSD. A single case-study was the best design because the approach would accomplished the research goals. Chapter three provided details of the recruitment process and protection of participants, as well as the theoretical sampling methods, and how the data from the study was analyzed.

Chapter 3

Research Method

The research study was a qualitative single case study in which open-ended questions in semi-structured interviews generated discussions to explore coping and adaptation in veteran army nurses with combat-related PTSD. A pilot sample was done with three veteran army nurses with combat-related PTSD, who met all inclusion criteria and who gave permission to audio-tape the interviews. The three pilot study participants were not included in the core sample. The 14 selected participants of the study were taken from a sample of 16 potential participants generated through the purposive, snowball sampling method. The pilot study participants who met all inclusion criteria were not included in the main study. Data extrapolation and analysis from transcribed interviews were accomplished with the assistance NVivo10. The pilot study resulted in the restructuring of the original research questions. The purpose of Chapter 3 was to discuss the research methodology identified for this study. The chapter included research method and design, appropriateness of design, research questions, the population, sampling frame, confidentiality, and informed consent. The geographic location, instrumentation, data collection, data analysis, validity and reliability, and summary completed the chapter.

Research Method and Design Appropriateness

The research method of choice for the study was qualitative. Of the various qualitative methodologies, the case study design was the most suitable for the study. Information from the research study helped to fill the gap in information about coping and adaptation among veteran army nurses with combat-related PTSD.

Qualitative Methodology

The core of qualitative inquiry is the ontological and epistemological perspective of constructivism and interpretivism (Neuman, 2006). Qualitative scholars posited that people pursue meaning and understanding of their world. Meaning is shaped by an individual's personal, cultural, beliefs, and background; consequently, meaning is diverse and complex. The goal of qualitative inquiry is to decode meaning and generate or expound patterns of meaning (Crotty, 1998; Lincoln & Guba, 1990; Neuman, 2006; Schwandt, 2007).

The quantitative research method was inappropriate for this study because quantitative research involves examining variables by collecting numerical data and statistically analyzing the data to test hypotheses. In contrast, the qualitative method involves the ability to explore processes and meanings that could not be quantified. The focus is on collecting and analyzing words, phrases, and sentences (Neuman, 2006). There was no apparent consensus on a specific sample size for qualitative studies; the guiding principle should be the concept of saturation (Mason 2010). In contrast, quantitative studies include large sample sizes so the findings have greater generalizability (Strauss & Corbin 2008).

Another advantage of qualitative research is the researcher has the ability to follow new ideas that emerge from the data (Charmaz, 2006). Qualitative analysis captures the complexity of reality through extensive data collection. Subsequent interpretations evolve by constant comparison of the data during the course of the study (Corbin & Strauss, 2015). The many concepts that emerge throughout the process of data collections, are connected to form links within the data. Qualitative research is frequently used in social and behavioral sciences to assist in the discovery of issues related to human behavior (Corbin & Strauss, 2015). The qualitative method in the study provided participants with a forum in which they could share personal experiences and perceptions to the open-ended questions.

Also, the qualitative method was appropriate for this study because the goal was to explore coping and adaptation from the perspective of veteran army nurses with combat-related PTSD. Qualitative methodology is appropriate when investigators want to understand phenomena from the perspectives of participants. People develop different subjective meanings of their experiences, and those differences and complexities of views are better understood within the confines of a qualitative method (Neuman, 2006). Use of the qualitative method elicited perceptions, influences, and attitudes that would not have emerged with a quantitative method.

Case Study Design.

This qualitative research study was conducted using a single-case study design. The case study design is suitable for investigating complex phenomena by studying a limited number of people, situations, or events in a bounded system (Hancock & Algozzine, 2011). The design is used when the objective is to analyze a single issue (Merriam, 2009; Stake, 2010; Yin, 2012), such as how veteran army nurses cope and adapt with combat-related PTSD.

Within the case study design, there are several different approaches that can be used, including exploratory, explanatory, instrumental, and intrinsic. The exploratory approach was most suitable for the study (Baxter & Jack, 2008). The exploratory approach consists of researching a phenomenon that has not been examined in depth.

Using this approach leads to findings that future investigators might use to conduct causal and further exploratory research (Streb, 2010). The exploratory approach was selected for this study because there was a lack of research on the coping and adaptation behaviors of veteran army nurses with combat-related PTSD. The exploratory approach was also suitable for the study because exploratory case research is flexible in regard to gathering data (Yin, 2012).

Case study research also has a focuses on a single case or multiple cases. The single-case focus involves investigating one person or group with similar characteristics and categorized in one bounded system (James, 2013). With the multiple-case focus, multiple distinct groups in different bounded systems are investigated and the results for the groups are compared (Houghton et al., 2013). The single case format was ideal for the study because the individuals recruited for the sample were members of one bounded system. Baxter and Jack (2008) also proposed binding the case to make certain the study remains reasonable in scope. To exclude the potential influences of extraneous variables and to bind the scope of the design, the study sample was limited to veteran army nurses with combat-related PTSD. Therefore, in this qualitative, single-case study, there was one unit of analysis, namely, veteran army nurses with combat-related PTSD who lived within a 30-mile radius of a military base located in the southwestern United States.

Research Questions

The research was conducted to explore how veteran army nurses with combat-related PTSD were coping and adapting. In alignment with the study's purpose, the investigation examined three research questions:

RQ1: How are veteran nurses coping and adapting after being diagnosed with combat-related PTSD?

RQ2: From the perspective of effective adaptation, what does coping and adapting with PTSD mean for veteran nurses?

RQ3: How does coping with PTSD affect the concept of self, the role of self in relation to others, and personal relationships?

Population and Geographic Location

The geographic location targeted for the study was a military base in the southwestern United States. The research population for the study comprised of male and female veteran army nurses with combat-related PTSD who were deployed in support of at least one of the Operation Enduring Freedom conflicts. Members of this population varied in age, culture and ethnicity.

Sample

The sample selection in qualitative research profoundly affects the quality of the research (Coyne, 2008). According to Neuman (2003), a sample represents a group of individuals smaller than the general research population, and who meet the same criteria as the research population. The sample for the study consisted of veteran army nurses with combat-related PTSD who were part of a population of military nurses diagnosed with PTSD. This population provided the greatest insight into the research questions.

Careful selection of research participants was necessary to ensure they met the inclusion criteria. In qualitative studies, several factors can determine sample sizes in contrast with quantitative studies. As a result, many researchers are reluctant to suggest what constitutes a sufficient sample size (Mason, 2010). However, Strauss and Corbin (2008) suggested that a small sample size is appropriate for qualitative research. A sample size of 5-15 participants was proposed for the study, and a sample of 14 was achieved.

Sampling Method

Purposive sampling was used to recruit participants for the study. Purposive sampling involves consciously selecting participants who meet the sample criteria and who were most likely to provide insights on the topic of study (Higginbottom, 2004). Purposive sampling was an appropriate sampling method for the study because the resulting participants contributed to a deeper understanding (Devers & Frankel, 2000) of how veteran army nurses with combat-related PTSD cope and adapt. Sometimes snowball sampling, which is asking a participant to suggest another participant, follows purposive sampling (Noy, 2008). Snowball sampling was successfully used to recruit additional participants.

Recruitment Strategy

A letter of support (Appendix I) for the study was secured from the Chief Nurse of the military treatment facility prior to requesting permission to post recruitment posters (Appendix J) and recruitment flyers (Appendix K). Verbal permission was received to post the flyers and posters. Flyers and posters were posted in the military treatment facility and two of its outlying clinics. The posters and flyers had the researcher's name and contact information, as well as a brief description of the study, time commitment, benefits of the study, and study criteria. Interested participants were invited to contact the researcher for more information.

Inclusion and Exclusion Criteria

Use of inclusion and exclusion criteria guided the selection of participants for the study. Inclusion criteria included (a) veteran army nurse of any race and gender, (b) deployment to Iraq or Afghanistan, or both, (c) in an active duty, retired, or separated status, (d) the willingness to self-disclose a diagnosis of combat-related PTSD, (e) ability to read, write, and speak English fluently, (f) be at least 18 years old; (g) no cognitive impairment, (h) live within a 30-mile radius of the target military base, and (i) be willing to discuss in an interview how they were coping and adapting. Exclusion criteria included participants who were unable to read or understand relative information or materials because of language or cognitive barriers; army reservists, members of other military branches, licensed practical nurses or combat medics. Deployment frequency was not an inclusion or exclusion criterion. Initial contact was initiated by each participant to express the desire to participate in the study.

Sample Size

The initial purposeful sampling method yielded 7 potential participants, which was adequate based on the proposed sample range of 5-15. However, in preparation for study drop-outs and to enhance the validity of the study's results, snowball sampling was used to recruit additional participants. Snowball sampling was suitable for the study because there is an extensive military community surrounding the selected military base, and participants would likely have connections with other individuals who met the inclusion criteria.

Snowball sampling yielded an additional 9 potential participants, bringing the sample total to 16. Of the 16 potential participants, 14 met all the inclusion criteria. Participant 15 was an army nurse in the reserved component and could not be included because inclusion criteria were active duty, retired, or separated veteran army nurses with combat-related PTSD. Participant 16 met all but one inclusion criteria, which was residing within the 30-mile radius of the military base. The participant resided outside the 30-mile radius and therefore was ineligible to participate. The 30-mile radius contained participants within the targeted military base.

Informed Consent

Research involving humans must adhere to practices rooted in ethical behaviors. Informed consent in research is consent given by knowledgeable potential participants to participate in a study without coercion, pressure, deception, fraud, or any inappropriate enticements (Berg, 2008). Obtaining informed consent is integral before collecting any data or study procedure (Banner & Zimmer, 2012). The practice of informed consent is based upon the principle that study participants are able to decide if it is in their best interest to participate in a research study of any kind, and that special protections are generally unnecessary for trauma-related studies (Newman & Kaloupek, 2009). Individuals who developed PTSD from a traumatic event are not inherently susceptible to coercion or impaired decision-making. Because of the nature of this study, it was imperative that each participant was not cognitively impaired, which they indicated on the demographic questionnaire.

After the 14 potential participants were verbally prescreened to determine qualification for the study, a letter of introduction (Appendix L) containing the purpose of the study, time commitment and requirements of the study was mailed to them. Following, an initial face-to-face meeting was convened with each participant separately in a private room at a community library on different dates. Permission to use the library (Appendix M) was secured prior to start of recruiting participants for the study. At each meeting, the participant again verbally verified his or her willingness to participate in the study, and signed the consent form (Appendix N). Participants were provided the option to take the consent form to review it. All participants declined this option. Prior to obtaining a signature, the consent form was reviewed and extensively discussed with each participant.

Information in the consent form included the voluntary nature of participation and procedures for withdrawal from the study. Entitlement to care and the potential risk for emotional distress were also discussed with participants. In addition to the informed consent, participants were also verbally informed that should they experience any discomfort during the interview, the interview would be terminated and resumed at a later date, or they could exercise their option of withdrawing from the study. Participants were also informed that in the event of such an experience, there was a licensed counselor on-call to assist them.

There were no withdrawals from the study. Data security and benefits of participation were also reviewed and discussed with each participant. Details of the non-disclosure agreement, (Appendix O) was explicitly stated in the consent form and was verbally reviewed with each participant. The signed non-disclosure agreement was secured from a licensed counselor prior to obtaining participants' consent to participate in the study. The counselor would have been available within 5 minutes of a phone call had there been a need. Participants identifying information was not shared with the counselor because none of the 14 participants experienced or reported any untoward effects during the interviews. If a participant had experienced any discomfort and the level of care was outside the scope of a licensed counselor, the participant would have been escorted to the nearest emergency room or a treatment facility for evaluation and safety. Entitlement to care was explicitly stated in the consent form.

After signing the informed consent each participant was provided with a link to Survey Monkey to access the demographic questionnaire and the PCL-M checklist. Based on self-disclosure information and the PCL-M scores, participants met the inclusion criteria of a diagnosis of PTSD. Information on the demographic survey indicated that participants were not cognitively impaired. After completion of both instruments, the researcher reviewed the responses to confirm all inclusion criteria were met. After confirmation, the interview times and dates were scheduled.

Confidentiality

Confidentiality is a crucial component in research involving humans. Participants should be assured that their participation would remain anonymous, and researchers must protect participants' anonymity to maintain a positive and trusting rapport (Berg, 2008). After obtaining informed consent, participants received a confidentiality agreement that indicated the participants' names and other personal information would not be disclosed to anyone. Their identity was protected with the use of pseudonyms, and interview transcripts were secured using an alphanumeric code. The pseudonyms were used for reporting the study results. All electronic documentation containing personal information, descriptions of personal characteristics, interview transcripts, tape recordings, and other content that could be linked to a participant's identity were stored on a personal computer with firewall password protection and a password protected external drive. Hard copy materials were stored in a file cabinet and secured under double lock at the researcher's residence. Destruction of the collected data and all study materials will occur no less than 3 years following completion of the study. At that time, all electronic files will be permanently deleted and hard copy materials will be shredded using a micro-cut shredder.

Data Collection

Data collection in the research study was accomplished through face-to-face interviews, and using open-ended questions to explore how veteran army nurses were coping and adapting with combat-related PTSD. A pilot study was also completed with three veteran army nurses with combat-related PTSD.

Pilot Study

Because the study's interview questions were not used in previous research, a pilot study was conducted to evaluate interview questions for clarity and validity. Pilot studies allow researchers to weigh, evaluate, and revise the data collection instrument to improve it (Yin, 2012; Hancock & Algozzine, 2011). Results from the pilot study provided insights to assist the researcher with the refinement of the data collection plan. The pilot testing process also helped the researcher determine whether questions were logical, understandable, and clear to participants (Yin, 2012). Pilot testing is a structured and effective method for receiving and recording preliminary data to discover aspects of the study that are in need of improvement (Neuman, 2003).

In accordance with the IRB requirements the three pilot study participants also signed consent forms and also gave permission for the interviews to be digitally recorded. The interviews were held in a private room at one of the local libraries. Interviews lasted between forty-five minutes to an hour and were digitally recorded, transcribed, and confirmed for accuracy. The pilot study was conducted over a three-day period yielding results that indicated some modification of the interview questions. An army nurse with a conferred doctoral degree was consulted in modification of the questions. Table 5 is a realignment of the 19 questions.

Table 5

Realignment of Interview Questions

Questions	Current Wording	Action	New Wording	Relation to RQs
Introductory Questions				
1	Tell me a little about yourself?	Keep as introduction to interview	No change	N/A
2	How long have you been a nurse?	Deleted	N/A	Not an inclusion criterion
3	How long have you been in the Army/separated from the Army/retired from the Army?	Deleted	N/A	Not an inclusion criterion
4	What dates were you deployed?	Moved to demographic questionnaire	No change	N/A
5	What conflict(s) were you deployed in support of?	Moved to demographic questionnaire	No change	N/A
6	Have you ever participated in a nursing research study before?	Deleted	N/A	Irrelevant to the study purpose
Interview Questions				
1	Were you directly or indirectly engaged in actual combat?	Deleted	N/A	Not an inclusion criterion
2	Describe what it was like for you in that situation	Deleted	N/A	Not directly related to the three main RQs (coping/ adapting, concept of self, and relationships with others
3	As a nurse, were there signs of PTSD that you could recognize in yourself?	Reworded and retained	What symptoms of PTSD, if any, did you recognized in yourself? When did you first notice these symptoms? (Interview question 1)	RQ 1 (Setting the stage/establishing the context for the interview questions)

93

#	Original Question	Action	Revised Question	RQ Mapping
4	Were you exhibiting these signs during the deployment?	N/A	N/A	Combined with RQ 1
5	At what phase of the deployment did you began seeing these signs?	N/A	N/A	Combined with RQ 1
6	How did you cope during this time?	Reworded and retained	How have you coped with and adapted to PTSD? (Interview question 3)	RQ 3
7	Did these symptoms affect your performance in any way?	Reworded and retained	How have these symptoms affected your performance, if at all, and are you doing anything to address the changes in your performance? (Interview question 2)	RQ 3
8	When were you medically diagnosed with PTSD related to your deployment?	Deleted	N/A	Irrelevant to research purpose
9	Are you still working as a nurse, and in what capacity?	Reworded and moved to demographic survey	Which of the following categories best describe your current status?	
10	How does having PTSD affect how you view yourself?	Reworded and retained	How does having PTSD affect your view of yourself? Why? (Interview question 5)	RQ 3
11	Does it affect your relationship with others? How? Why?	Reworded and retained	How does having PTSD affect your relationship with others? Why? (Research question 6)	RQ 3
12	How are you coping and adapting with PTSD?	N/A	N/A	Combined with RQ 1
13	What is coping and adaptation from your perspective?	Reworded and retained	In terms of experiencing PTSD, what do coping and adapting mean and what is involve? (Interview question 4)	RQ 2

Main Study

The primary method for collecting data was through in-depth, face-to-face, semi-structured interviews. The interviews were scheduled after consent forms were secured and eligibility confirmed. No interviews were conducted until the pilot study was completed and interview questions were finalized. The interview times were set based on the participants' availability. In accordance with the IRB requirements all 14 study participants signed consent forms and gave permission for the interviews to be digitally recorded. The interviews were held in a private room at the local library. Each interview lasted from 45 to 60 minutes.

During the semi-structured interviews, participants were encouraged to ask for clarification if they did not understand any of the questions. Preliminary introductions helped participants feel at ease so they were more willing to candidly share how they were coping and adapting with PTSD, particularly by describing specific examples of coping and adaptation (Kvale, 2009). After the preliminary introductions, the interviews continued with the research questions. During each interview a licensed counselor was on call to assist a participant who experienced any emotional discomfort. The counselor was also available to the three pilot study participants. As previously stated, none of the 14 participants reported or demonstrated any signs of emotional discomfort; therefore, the licensed counselor never interacted with any participant. Participants' identifying information was not revealed to the counselor. Data collection via participant interviews continued until data saturation was reached. A diagram of the main study collection process is depicted in (Figure 3).

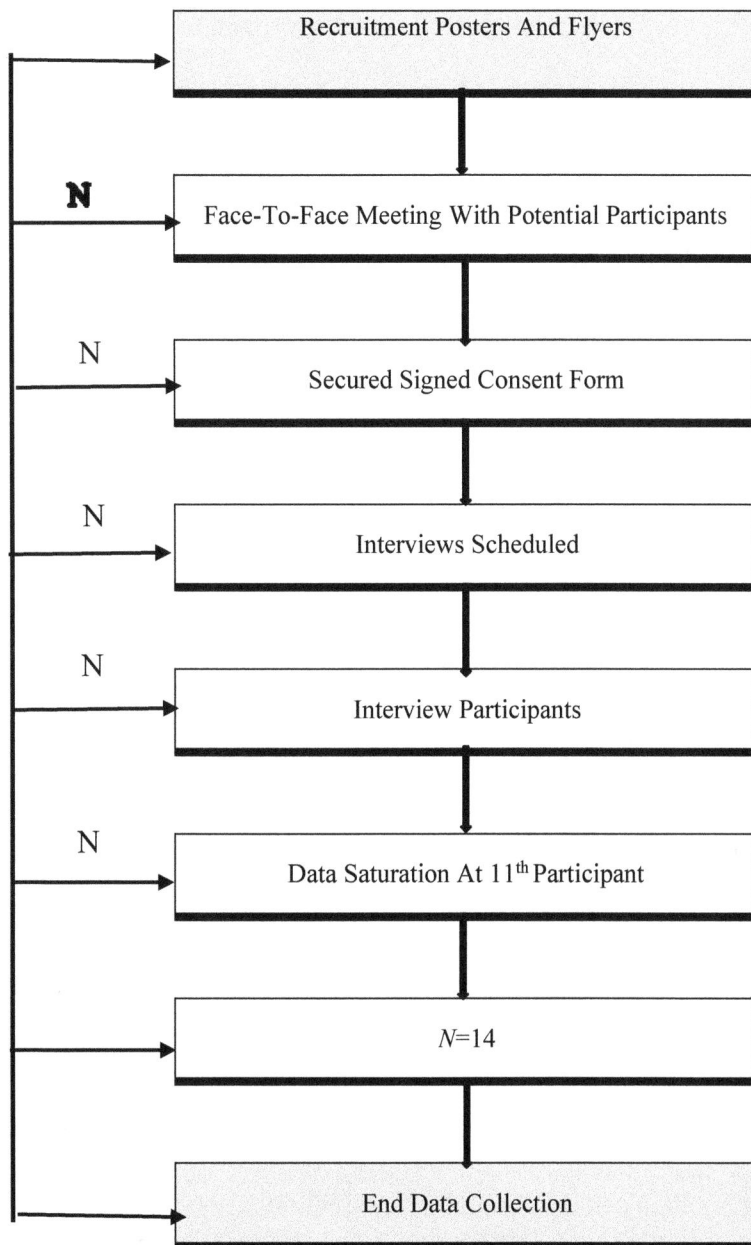

Figure 3. Main study collection process.

Data Saturation

Data saturation is considered the most accurate approach to ensure sufficient, quality data are obtained (Merriam, 2009; Walker, 2012). Failure to achieve data saturation can impact the quality and content validity of a research study. Data saturation is achieved when there is enough information to replicate the study, when there is no additional new information, and when continued coding is no longer feasible (Fusch & Ness, 2015). After each interview, preliminary analysis was done to identify any new themes and topics. Interviews were conducted until data saturation was verified. Data saturation occurred for the study when new data did not alter the themes discovered. For the study, data saturation was achieved after interviewing the 11th participant. To verify and evaluate whether data saturation had been achieved, the data was again reviewed to identify patterns and repetition in the responses, as well as any new topics.

Instrumentation

There are several approaches to collecting data for research. In qualitative research, interviews, observations, and document analysis are general approaches. Instrumentation is critical in qualitative and quantitative research. The researcher as instrument can sometimes be a threat to trustworthiness in qualitative research. However, the researcher as instrument is central to conducting qualitative research (Chenail, 2011).

Researcher as Instrument

Qualitative research allows the researcher to interact with study participants, which provides the opportunity to gather raw words as well as the ability to document non-verbal responses and cues. As participants and researchers interact, relationships are formed (Brodsky, 2008). In this qualitative study the goal was to explore coping and adaptation in veteran army nurses with combat-related PTSD. To accomplish the goal, it was necessary for the researcher to understand the concepts from the participants' perspective. Therefore, the researcher was an instrument gathering, analyzing, and interpreting the data to reach a conclusion.

Self-Disclosure

Self-disclosure is a process whereby individuals reveal personal and intimate feelings, thoughts, beliefs, and attitudes about oneself. The process of self-disclosure could help in building rapport between the researcher and the participant, especially when disclosing sensitive information (Dickson-Swift, James, Kippen, & Liamputtong, 2009). Self-disclosure of PTSD was the primary inclusion criteria for selection of participants. This study, the research questions, and the method used to answer the questions were strictly qualitative. Two quantitative measures were utilized to validate participants' disclosure of PTSD. For the purpose of this study participants did not need to have active symptoms of PTSD at the time of their interview.

Quantitative Measures

The demographic questionnaire and the PCL-M checklist were the two quantitative measures used. The demographic sheet was a16-item questionnaire developed to solicit responses specifically related to the inclusion criteria, and the PCL-M checklist was a 17-item self-report tool used to validate participants' report of PTSD. The checklist is a government document in the public domain and did not require permission to use. All 14 participants received a score greater than 50 (the minimum required for a positive result) on the PCL-M. The scores ranged from 56–72. The 6 interview questions were open ended. The open-ended questions and semi-structured format were appropriate for qualitative research where the goal is to understand a phenomenon from the participants' perspectives (Denzin & Lincoln, 2008; Merriam, 2009).

Semi-Structured Interviews

Semi-structured interviews were another instrument used in the study. The interviews were conducted from the perspective of what Kvale and Brinkmann (2009) called "knowledge as produced," which suggested researchers view the research interview as a production site of knowledge. This knowledge is developed from the interaction between interviewer and interviewee and is accomplished through questions and answers. The interviewer and interviewee takes ownership of the product. The production process is maintained throughout the different phases from transcription to reporting and the reported knowledge is mixed with the methods and techniques used along the way (Kvale & Brinkmann, 2009). To ensure participants' information was accurately transcribed, interviews were digitally recorded with their permission. After all 14 participants were interviewed, data collection for the study was closed.

Credibility

Credibility refers to the selection of participants and confidence in the data collection and analysis processes (Graneheim & Lundman, 2004). Credibility in the study was achieved by selecting participants who met the sample criteria that were established to achieve the purpose of the research. Because the researcher is an active duty registered nurse who supported one of the three conflicts and has combat-related PTSD, it was necessary to maintain credibility of information. The researcher was conscious about personal thoughts and the influence of those thoughts on the data

100

collection and data analysis processes. The researcher consistently reflected on the role of a researcher, which is to conduct research utilizing objective methods and procedures.

Participation was not limited to individuals of a specific gender, ethnicity, or cultural background; the diversity among the participants illuminated the various coping and adapting strategies. Credibility in the analysis process was established by selecting relevant coding units and including only relevant data, through the use of NVivo10, a qualitative data analysis program that helped to reduce errors during the analysis process.

To further maintain credibility, participants verified the accuracy of their interview transcripts, corrected any errors, and clarified any concepts as appropriate. To strengthen credibility, interview transcripts and the researcher's notes were compared in an effort to establish the congruence or incongruence of the findings in this study. Peer debriefing is another approach to establishing credibility in qualitative research (Lincoln & Guba, 1990). Three experts in the area of study were consulted to perform peer debriefing. Each expert reviewed three transcripts as well as the researcher's notes for data validation.

Dependability

Dependability is comparable to reliability in quantitative research. Dependability relates to variability in the research environment; this variability is one of the many challenges of qualitative research. Dependability can be increased through becoming familiar with appropriate research protocols and then applying them in the study (Jensen, 2008). Dependability in the study was established through an audit trail that included details of the study procedures and the data collection and analysis processes.

Transferability

Transferability is the process by which the research findings can be transferred to other groups or settings (Polit & Beck, 2004). Transferability aligns with external validity and generalizability in quantitative research (Shenton, 2004). For the findings to be transferable, the study sample, the location of the study, and the context of the study must be explained in detail (Graneheim & Lundman, 2004). This single-case study maintained transferability by providing adequate contextual information regarding location of the study, participation criteria, and reporting a rich description of the studied phenomenon. Information included (a) background data, (b) existing phenomenon knowledge, (c) target research area, (d) sample inclusions and exclusions, (e) sample size ($n=14$), (f) data collection methods, and (g) duration of interview sessions (Shenton, 2004). Participants' demographics were presented in chapter 4.

After digital audio-recordings were downloaded and transcribed, the researcher reviewed the transcripts several times to check for accuracy. Using the United States Postal Services registered mail return receipt option, participants were provided with a printed copy of their interview to further verify accuracy of the digital transcription. Attached to each transcript was a letter with instructions to the participant (Appendix P). Each participant was asked to return the transcript with written feedback to the researcher within 5 days. Participants verified their interviews for accuracy and returned all interviews within 5 days. This process promoted reliability and trustworthiness. After all corrections were made, and quality was confirmed, data analysis began. Data was analyzed via content analysis.

Content Analysis

Content analysis is one of the numerous approaches for analyzing qualitative data, and it has been used in several studies on nursing. Content analysis is a scientific tool for obtaining new insights, increasing understanding of a phenomenon, and forming practical actions. Additionally, content analysis can be used to strengthen and expand current theory (Hsieh & Shannon, 2005). The researchers identified three distinct approaches within qualitative content analysis: directed, conventional, and summative. The differences in the approaches are primarily in the schemes used for codes, origins of codes, and threats to trustworthiness. The directed approach is a deductive application that enables researchers to decide on the primary coding scheme, the connections between codes, and on which connections to focus. Conventional content analysis is an inductive application in which the investigator is immersed in the data, allowing new insights to emerge. Summative content analysis can be inductive or deductive and involves quantifying words in the text (Hsieh & Shannon, 2005; Mayring, 2000; Schreier, 2012). The deductive approach was used in the study.

The investigator's interests and the issue being studied determines which content analysis approach is most appropriate for a study. The deductive approach is used when there is existing theory that may be validated or extended based on the research data, which is primarily collected through interviews and open-ended questions (Granheim & Lundman, 2004; Hsieh & Shannon, 2005). Deductive content analysis was more appropriate for the study because this approach provided a basis for RAM to be conceptually substantiated, expanded, or modified.

Both inductive and deductive content analysis consists of three main phases: (1) preparation where the unit of analysis is defined, as well as making sense of the data, (2) organization of the data depending on the content analysis approach, and (3) reporting of the study results. A diagram (Figure 4), is a summary of the phases.

Preparation.

Preparation begins with selecting or defining the unit of analysis. In case study terminology, *unit of analysis* refers to the case being studied (Baxter & Jack, 2008); in content analysis terminology, the term refers to the form the analysis results will take. The unit must be defined before messages can be coded (Elo & Kyngas, 2007). The unit of analysis in the study was the transcribed interviews. All sounds and pauses in response to the interview questions were included in the transcription. During the preparation phase, the researcher attempted to make sense of the data by reading the transcripts several times, and repeatedly listening to the audiotapes.

Organization of Data.

The process of organizing the data is dependent upon the approach that is used. If an inductive approach is used, the next step in the organization phase includes open coding, grouping, categorization, and abstraction. If a deductive content analysis approach is used the next step is developing a categorization matrix and code the data according to the categories (Elo & Kyngas, 2007). A categorization matrix (Table 6) was developed, and the data reviewed for content and coded according to the modes of RAM used in this study. NVivo 10 was used to assist with the coding and analyzing of data for emergent themes and connections.

Table 6

Categorization Matrix

Modes	Adaptive Responses	Ineffective Responses
Self-Concept	"We are less afraid."	"I feel like a loser."
	"I slip into that meditation mode when I get anxious.	"At first I was very embarrassed."
	"I couldn't cope without prayers."	"I couldn't even do my job."
Role Function	"I'm gonna make sure my family is good."	"I can't even be a real husband or father."
	"I was doing what I love."	"I'm afraid of a committed relationship."
	"But my wife stood by me."	
Interdependence	We know we can count on … family and extended family."	"I'm mostly by myself at work."
	"With friends and my husband, I have a good support."	"PTSD does affect my relationship with others."

Reporting the Results.

The final step in the content analysis process is reporting the results. The results of the research were reported in chapter 4. Based on the theoretical framework, the results indicated that veteran army nurses with combat-related PTSD were at the compensatory adaptation level. According to Merriam (2009), categories of data should respond to the research purpose, and be consistent and practical (Merriam, 2009). In the study, relationships were formed from the information collected during the interviews; predominant themes were uncovered and explained. Insights and conclusions were derived from the data analysis. An important aspect of qualitative analysis is discovering the meaning of the data (Merriam, 2009). To enhance explanation and interpretation of collected data the inclusion of confidentially-coded quotes from interviews were

presented in Chapter 4.

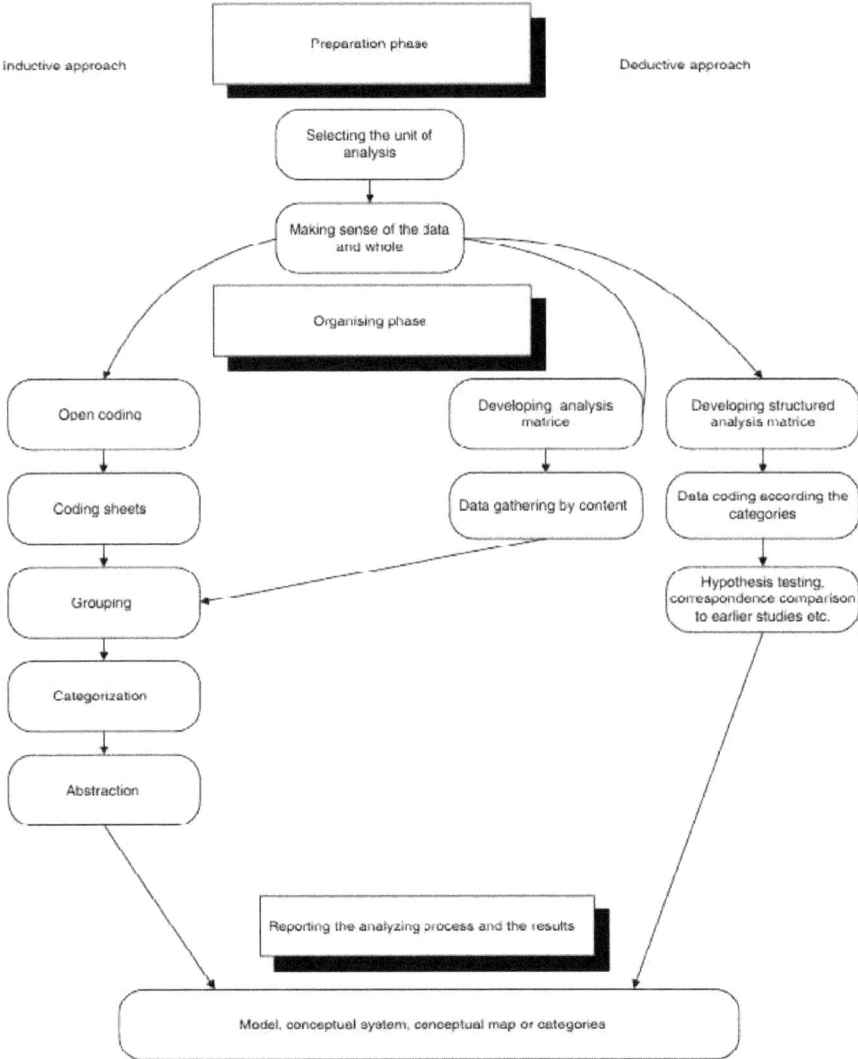

Inductive approach

Deductive approach

Preparation phase

Selecting the unit of analysis

Making sense of the data and whole

Organising phase

Open coding

Developing analysis matrice

Developing structured analysis matrice

Coding sheets

Data gathering by content

Data coding according the categories

Grouping

Hypothesis testing, correspondence comparison to earlier studies etc.

Categorization

Abstraction

Reporting the analyzing process and the results

Model, conceptual system, conceptual map or categories

Figure 4. Phases in the content analysis process.

Summary

Chapter 3 contained the details of the study method, including descriptions of the research method and design and the justification for selecting them. The research questions were presented, and the population, sample, and sampling method were discussed. Also presented were the informed consent process and methods that were applied to ensure confidentiality. The chapter additionally contained discussion of the data collection instrument and method, qualitative validity, and the data analysis process.

The qualitative method and single-case design were used to direct the study. Purposive sampling was used to recruit 14 participants who met the criteria of (a) veteran army nurse of any race and gender; (b) deployment to Iraq or Afghanistan (c) active duty, retired, or separated status; (d) self-disclosed a diagnosis of PTSD as a result of deployment; (e) ability to read, write, and speak English; (f) be at least 18 years old; (g) no cognitive impairment; (h) live within a 30-mile radius of the targeted military base, and be willing to discuss their experiences and coping and adapting strategies in an interview. Data were collected through semi-structured interviews with open-ended questions. This data collection method gave participants the opportunity to tell their stories in their own words (Lincoln & Guba, 1990). Content analysis with NVivo 10 was used to code the data and identify themes regarding how veteran army nurses with combat-related PTSD cope and adapt. Chapter 4 contains a summary of the sample and the results of the study.

Chapter 4

Results

The purpose of this qualitative single case study was to explore how veteran army nurses are coping and adapting with combat-related PTSD. Chapter 4 includes a review of the research process, including participant recruitment, the pilot study, the semi-structured interviews with open-ended questions, and the data analysis process. The chapter also contains demographic information on the 14 participants, followed by a presentation of the three major themes identified through analyzing the data. Thirteen interview questions were developed on the basis of the three research questions in addition to six introductory questions. After the pilot, all 19 questions were revised and six retained for the main study. The remaining questions were either eliminated or added to the demographic questionnaire.

Pilot Study

Prior to the main study, a pilot study was completed with three veteran army nurses with combat-related PTSD and who met all other inclusion criteria. In accordance with Institutional Review Board requirements, the three pilot study participants signed the informed consent and gave permission for the interviews to be digitally recorded. The pilot study interviews were held in a private room at a local library. The interviews were conducted over the span of three days, with 45 to 60 minutes in duration. Interviews were digitally recorded, transcribed, and member checked for accuracy. The participants answered the 19 interview questions and had the opportunity to provide feedback on the questions and the interview process. The feedback indicated the need to decrease the number of interview questions. Some of the questions were combined, some questions were deleted, and other questions were added to the demographic questionnaire. After the modifications, six open-ended questions remained for the interviews. As the final step in the pilot study, an army nurse with a doctoral degree reviewed and validated the six questions.

Data Collection

Following the pilot study, data collection in the main study began. Each interview started with a brief introduction, a review of the informed consent, a brief explanation of the interview approach, and a request for permission to audiotape the interview. Each participant verbally granted permission in addition to the informed consent, to record the interview. Audiotaped interviews promoted accurate documentation of the participants' responses as well as pauses, vocal inflections, and other verbal cues that might provide insight during the analysis process.

Following the introductory formalities, when the participant was ready, he or she was asked the six open-ended questions. Each participant had the opportunity to ask for clarification of the questions if needed. The interview questions were based on the research questions and were designed to explore in depth how veteran army nurses with combat-related PTSD cope and adapt.

During the interviews, notes were taken to summarize responses and document nonverbal cues. Some of the topics the participants discussed were sensitive. Nevertheless, the participants provided detailed, personal responses to the questions, which were phrased in general terms with probing questions as needed. Participants were informed that they were not required to answer any of the questions, and if they experienced any distress, they could take a break from the interview or end the interview.

After each interview was completed the researcher also reminded each participant of the probability of feeling more stressed after divulging information about a traumatic event. Participants were encouraged to call the interviewer if they experienced any distressing emotional reactions. No participant contacted the researcher.

Interviews were conducted until data saturation was verified. To evaluate whether data saturation had been achieved, after each interview the data were reviewed to identify patterns and repetition in the responses, as well as any new topics that were not fully developed and therefore needed more exploration. Completing this process indicated that data saturation was achieved after conducting the 11th interview. Three additional interviews were conducted to verify data saturation.

Data Analysis

After the interviews were completed, the researcher transcribed the recordings without the use of a third party. The transcribed data amounted to 250 typed pages. Each transcription was saved in a separate Microsoft Word document. The audio recording and transcripts were compared twice to ensure the accuracy of the transcriptions. The participants also member checked their transcripts to ensure accuracy. The data were examined using content analysis.

The purpose of the analysis process was to make sense of the data by consolidating it, organizing it into categories, and identifying themes regarding the participants' experiences and perceptions. To assist in the analysis, the transcripts were imported into NVivo 10. The analysis process began by identifying topics that would likely appear in the data; these topics were used as initial codes. In NVivo, relevant interview data were assigned codes. Additional codes were identified and assigned based on further reviewing the data. Irrelevant data were removed from the analysis. The coded data were grouped into nodes, or categories, and then the nodes were repeatedly reviewed to identify patterns. The contents of each node were reviewed numerous times to understand how they related and to identify major themes across the participants' interview responses. The resulting three themes consisted of multiple nodes with data from several participants.

Participant Demographics

The population from which the sample was drawn from was within a 30-mile radius of a military base in the southwestern United States. The sample size consisted of 14 veteran army nurses with combat-related PTSD. Participants ages ranged from 20 years to 50 years (Mean = 36 years). There were 8 females (57.1%), and 6 males (43%). The sample consisted of 7 African Americans (50%); 5 Caucasians (36.1%); and 2 Hispanics (14.2%). Nine participants were retired (64.2%); 3 fulfilled their obligation or were separated otherwise from the military (21.4%); and 2 were still on active duty (14.2%). Regarding participants' deployment status, 3 were deployed to both Iraq and Afghanistan; (21.4%); 10 were deployed to Iraq only (71.4%), and 1 was deployed to Afghanistan only (7.1%). A summary of the sample demographics (Table 7) is presented in the following section.

Table 7

Summary of Participants Demographics

Sample Characteristics	N	Percentages
Gender		
Female	8	57.1%
Male	6	43%
Race		
Black/African American	7	50%
White/Caucasian	5	36.1%
Hispanic/Latino	2	14.2%
Current Military Status		
Retired	9	64.2%
Active Duty	2	14.2%
Fulfill Obligation or Otherwise Separated	3	21.4%
Areas of Deployment		
Iraq	10	71.4%
Afghanistan	1	7.1%
Both Iraq and Afghanistan	3	21.4%

Presentation Findings

Analyzing the interview data resulted in the identification of three main themes. These themes including the percentages of responses (Figure 5) are presented in the following subsections. Quotes from the interviews are included to provide support for the themes.

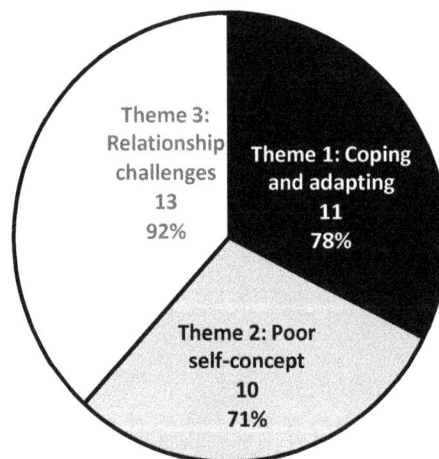

Figure 5. Number of participants mentioning each theme.

Theme 1: Strategies for Coping and Adapting.

The first theme, Strategies for coping, relates to the first and second research questions, regarding coping and adaptation with PTSD, and what constitutes effective adaptation from participants' perspective.

1.   RQ1: How are veteran nurses coping and adapting after being diagnosed with combat-related PTSD?

2.   RQ2: From the perspective of effective adaptation, what does coping and adapting with PTSD mean for veteran nurses?

In the interviews, the participants explained that they used many strategies to cope with and adapt to PTSD. These strategies include praying and engaging in other religious practices, seeking support from family and friends, drinking, avoiding situations that would likely prompt memories of the traumatic experience, practicing yoga and meditating, and remaining busy. Participants typically used more than one of these strategies.

Prayer and religion. According to the data analysis, the most common strategies were prayer and religious beliefs. Eight participants (57%) discussed using these strategies to cope because of the sense of peace and strength this approach offered. Also, the use of prayer and religion to cope was seemingly an unconscious response, and one that brought comfort, and provided a way to accept the daily challenges of PTSD.

According to Cece "Coping? I really don't even know how I'm coping. I guess I would say with a lot of prayers and acceptance of where my life is right now."

Another participant, Julia also discussed how her strong faith enabled her to accept the diagnosis of PTSD and helped her and her family overcome the most difficult times:

When we get sidetracked, God sometimes puts us in situations where we have to go back to our faith. Outside of that, we are powerless to deal with things in our lives. So I couldn't cope without prayers and a relationship with God, and my husband couldn't deal with me without his connection with God. I really don't see any other way for us to deal with this issue of PTSD. Now, our spiritual dependence has gotten better and . . . although we are still dealing with the symptoms of PTSD, we are less afraid. We know we can count on our church family and extended family to pray us up when I have a bad day.

Mary also discussed the role of faith in ability to cope with PTSD:

I just take it one day at a time now and leave the rest to God—faith without works is dead, so I can't just leave it up to God and do nothing. . . . I have to do my part, and it's doing all these things and exercising my faith in him.

Mark emphasized the need to pray and meditate to cope with PTSD:

I think the biggest thing that help[s] me to cope is I meditate, you know. I meditate and pray a lot. Men with all our macho persona and all that mask—we don't wanna admit to things, you know, but the older I get, I realize there is more to life than just self.

Karen also discussed prayer:

For me, what has worked and still works is prayer. . . . I had to get a spiritual grip on my life and on everything, you know? Believe me, you need strength to deal

114

with what is going on in the mind—it's crazy. So prayer . . . is helping me to

cope with PTSD.

Olivia reported that her church family helps her cope with PTSD:

I'm very active in my church. . . . Church plays a heavy role in my healing. My

church family surrounded us [her family] with love and, you know, prayer when I

first accepted the diagnosis of PTSD and decided to deal with it.

Family and friends. Six of the participants (42%) discussed relying on family

and friends to help them cope with their illness. While this approach can sometimes be

difficult for individuals providing support, social and familial support are oftentimes the

main support for individuals who are faced with terminal illnesses and chronic mental

illnesses such as PTSD. The person with PTSD are sometimes more comfortable talking

about the traumatic events with families and friends.

Trisha emphasized the impact of a strong support system:

It's who or what you have for your support system and how effective it is. You

know, if you have a good support system to help you through any crisis, then I

think you might be able to cope with the issue, but it is different for everyone. I

would say with friends and my husband I have a good support system.

Olivia agreed, stating that "family is very important when you['re] trying to adjust and

deal with . . . this diagnosis of PTSD." Similarly, Mary discussed the support she

receives from her family, particularly her husband:

He's in the military still, so he understands my diagnosis and so he's been a great

sense of support for me as far as understanding if I don't want go with a crowd or,

you know, I don't wanna sit with my back to the door or anything like that, he

understands. . . . My boys are no longer at home, but they visit often and they call
to check on me, and sometimes their voices are just what I need to hear for that
particular time. So family is definitely important, be it church family, immediate
family or extended family.

John also shared how he wanted to be better for his wife and baby girl because his
wife stood by him through all of his experience:

At first I didn't even want to face that I have PTSD. I just wanted to do my time
and retire like I'm supposed to. I gave up—seriously. I just said, "Man, I can't
deal with this crap." A man is supposed to take care of his family and [be] strong,
you know, and I just wasn't that at all. . . . But my wife stood by me. She never
left my side.

His wife's support motivated him to cope with PTSD so he could be a strong husband
and father:

I don't want my wife and baby girl see me and feel like, you know, like I'm weak
and all that . . . and I can't deal with things. I gotta set the example. I'm gonna
make sure my family is good.

Drinking. Strategies for coping and adaptation was the first theme that emerged
from the data, which answered RQ 1 and RQ 2. Five participants (36%) mentioned
drinking to cope with PTSD. Different individuals approach situations differently.
While some use positive coping skills, others may use strategies that are less desirable
such as alcohol, and or substance abuse to help decrease or eliminate physical pain or
mental anguish. The participants were healthcare providers who were taking prescribed

116

psychiatric medication. However, there were no verbal or non-verbal indication that they were concerned about any possible interaction between the medication and alcohol.

Viola said she destresses and deals with PTSD by drinking with her friends: "Hanging out with my friends and taking a drink every now and then help me to relax and cope with this PTSD." Another participant, Heidi, noted that she has a few drinks when she feels the need to do so:

> Of course, I am taking my medication and still going to counselling for it [PTSD], but I take a couple of drinks when I feel overly anxious and scared and when I get the flashbacks. I am what you might call a "closet drinker." I don't smoke or anything, but I take a couple glasses of wine perhaps more than I should, you know? I deny it each time I see my counselor, and there is no way she can prove otherwise. So I guess you can say my coping strategy is to drink a little bit more than I should. I don't run and hide from the problem, but I basically drink to forget.

As with Heidi, Olivia also drank but did not want friends and family to know:

"I must admit . . . that in addition to all this support [from family] I am what you would call a closet drinker." Trisha likewise admitted that despite a strong support system, "None of these people know I take a few extra glasses of wine." Felix reluctantly explained that he "take[s] a couple drinks. Nothing to make me intoxicated, but just to numb the pain."

Avoidance. Three participants (21%) coped and adapted by avoiding situations that would remind them of their traumatic experiences, and stay busy to forget their experiences. Avoidance, as well as alcohol are considered inadequate or safe coping

117

strategies. Oftentimes with PTSD, individuals try to avoid reliving the traumatic experience by avoiding anything or anyone that brings back the memories. For some, this strategy can sometimes decrease the emotional pain.

Kyle shared the following.

I definitely don't watch anything on TV that reminds me of downrange and the stuff I seen. Every time I see something that reminds me of some of the things I saw there, I get freaked out. For real! Because [for] the next week or two is like I'm watching a slide show just keep repeating in my head and then I can't sleep, you know. It's rough.

Oscar, hesitantly explained how and why he avoided certain people and situations:

We had translators around the hospital, of course, to help us with understanding the locals, and I tell ya, I couldn't stand for them to be around because the guys would tell you how they got injured, you know? Some kid or woman standing by all innocent and shit, and before you know it, *boom*! I wasn't out there in the heat of the battle, but as nurses we get them back messed up, and it's as if we were actually the ones out there. To this day, I don't like people wearing covers on their head and faces. Don't get me wrong, I respect every religion, but seeing that in my own country sometimes scares me. I get anxious and panic, you know. I know pretty soon I can go and enjoy all movies with my buddies, but for now I just chill and watch them from home. That way I can fast forward what I don't want to see and don't feel like anybody is judging me.

Another participant used avoidance as a coping skill by running away from the problem and remaining busy:

I don't mean I literally run away, but you know, getting busy without doing anything really. You know, just doing busy work without any real goal. You just do it to pretend the problem don't exist. . . . I will just get up and drive to _____ just to get out the house. I play golf and basketball and sometime shoot some pool, you know, anything to keep me busy and take my mind off the shit that just keep on coming and clouding my mind. It's scary as hell.

Yoga and meditation. Two participants (14%) reported the use of yoga and meditation as their coping strategy. Yoga and meditation are techniques that are sometimes used for stress relief and anxiety, which co-exists with PTSD. The premise of yoga is to help the individual access his or her inner strength. When coupled with breathing techniques, relaxation, and meditation, it has been known to help the individual build coping skills. Luke appeared shy when he mentioned practicing yoga. When asked if he was reticent to elaborate on his response, he replied:

"Hell yea." Chuckling, he explained that "guys are not really into that sorta thing." He then described how he used yoga, relaxation, and reflection to cope with PTSD:

We [he and his fiancée] joined a yoga class about 10 minutes from the house, and we would take classes like every Mondays, Wednesdays, and Fridays. . . . I have to say it really helps, you know, but at first I felt like a little sissy going to a yoga class. But surprisingly, men were in that class and I didn't feel too bad. . . . Me and my fiancée, we also did some meditation stuff. I tell ya, she really believed in

119

that stuff, and it worked. I find now that I slip into that meditation mode when I get anxious.

Theme 2: Poor Self-concept.

The second theme was related to the third research question: How does coping with PTSD affect the concept of self, the role of self in relation to others, and personal relationships? The participants believed that PTSD contributed to low self-esteem, self-blame, and weakness.

Low self-esteem. Eight participants (57%) indicated they struggled with low self-esteem. Mental illness has been stigmatized by society. Those who suffer with mental illness must carry the burden of the illness as well as the stigma associated with it, which can sometimes cause isolation for fear of being rejected by society. This stigma also exists in the Military. For most soldiers in the Army the goal is to retire after serving 20 years or more with a honorable discharge. When the soldier is discharged for reasons other than voluntary retirement, there can be a sense of failure, especially if the discharge was due to PTSD or other mental illness. Mark among others, was medically discharged, which made him feel worthless with a sense of failure. Mark articulated:

> At first I thought I was a loser—no, really. I couldn't even do my job, and it was hard to fit . . . in - to be a nurse again without bullets flying all around you. When I was deployed, I felt like I punked out when my team needed me most. Then you know how the military have this stigma about mental health? I felt like I was such a loser and that I couldn't even do my job. I had to depend on medication and sitting in a shrink chair to talk about my feelings and issues.

Viola also admitted feeling embarrassed to be diagnosed with PTSD. Additionally, she was ashamed that she drank as a coping mechanism:

> At first I was very embarrassed to hear I have PTSD. I thought everything was my fault, and I still think so. Then there is the drinking. I would be the first to tell patients alcohol don't and won't solve their problems, but here is me, you know, miss goody two shoes, messing up myself instead of facing the problem. Sometimes I feel so useless.

Luke likewise indicated he had low self-esteem because of PTSD. In particular, his diagnosis made him feel weak:

> I see myself as a little sissy, you know, not being able to face the fact that, yes, men do get PTSD like any other illness and that's perfectly normal. Not that it's normal to get PTSD, but if you go to war it's bound to happen. Someone will be affected by what they see or by their environment, but I just think it should not have to be me—hey, I'm a man. We deal with things head-on, but I guess not being able to see an illness—you know, a mental illness—you can't see it, so you can't fight it and deal with it head-on.

Mary explained how her low self-esteem was effecting her performance in her current job:

> I feel that the time I was sitting home and being depressed and all that was time I should be spending doing my job. Sometimes every now and then I second-guess myself, especially when I have to medicate a patient. Sometimes even now I get flashbacks about how inadequate I felt then and whether I was sane enough to give this patient medication or talk them through any crisis.

Karen likewise doubted her work-related competencies:

> When I had to get out of the army that was not easy for me to accept because not only was I a nurse, but I was a soldier with other soldiers reporting to me. I was terrified because . . . I had been out of the clinical realm, so to speak, so I didn't deal with the medical side directly but more indirectly. I was afraid I would have a hard time finding a job, especially one where I would be asked to deal with patients who are mental or who have PTSD, whether from the military or some other experience in their lives. I just didn't think I could handle that anymore and be sane and basically being civilized and not feeling unsafe. Then that made me feel like I was not a whole person and that something was wrong with me—that I was not normal.

John discussed doubt about his professional and personal abilities, particularly if he did not use pharmaceutical drugs:

> I sometimes think I made a mistake joining the Army, that I made a mistake becoming a nurse and trying to help people, because right now I don't feel like I'm in a position to help anyone. Heck, not even myself. But it gets worse when I gotta look at my wife and child and feel like I let them down, you know, like I can't even be a real husband or father. . . . That's the hardest part I see . . . when I look at myself.

Self-blame. Although a low number of participants mentioned self-blame, this can also viewed as overlapping with low self-esteem. Two participants (14%) mentioned self-blame. It is not unusual for an individuals to blame self, especially if they perceived themselves as a failure, as well as being powerless. One participant Viola, blamed herself for what she thought was her fault. She felt that her role as a nurse was to provide care to others, but found herself in an environment where she doubted her ability to provide care.

> Every day I blame myself. . . . I thought that as a nurse going to support the troops that I was doing what I love - taking care of soldiers - but after my first deployment I was like this is too much. How can any human see the things that we have to see and deal with those things every day all day and still be normal? Whenever I would lose a patient, I would question my care. Did I do this? . . . I blamed myself for everything that went wrong. Every soldier our hospital lost— everything. I internalized it, and I blamed myself. To this day, I still struggle with . . . blaming myself.

Heidi also blamed herself for problems at work:

> I thought I was a total crazy, wacko person that should be locked away before she causes harm to herself and others. . . . What I can tell you, though, is that even though I think I am getting better at this, back then I felt like . . . everything was my fault. I felt like I was to be blamed if the shift didn't go as planned or if something didn't get done or get done on time.

Theme 3: Relationship Challenges.

The third theme was also related to the third research question: How does coping with PTSD affect the concept of self, the role of self in relation to others, and personal relationships? The participants discussed several ways in which PTSD affected relationships.

Avoidance of socialization and misrepresentation. Seven participants (50%) indicated that because of PTSD, they avoided socializing with others. In conjunction with withdrawing socially, some participants also withheld information or purposefully misled others. Because of these three actions, the participants experienced strains in relationships with family, friends, and colleagues. Some relationships were even terminated.

Trisha explained that because of PTSD, sometimes she did not want to be around other people:

> There are still anger issues that I am dealing with, and I still get depressed, and when that type of feelings gets to be overwhelming, I withdraw. I don't do small talk, and I'm mostly by myself at work. And being a case manager works well for me because I'm in my own office and most of my clients are through the hospital referral, and then I only get to meet with them at time of discharge and maybe one or two times after, so that serves me well. I am getting much better at it, but I limit my trips to the grocery store because if the cashier line is too long, I get frustrated and angry. If someone accidentally bounces me with a shopping cart, I am ready to go off. That's not good, and it definitely is a rude and negative response to my environment. My kids are away from home . . . and I love to hear their voices at times, but they told their dad that sometimes they call and they can hear the aloofness and it makes them feel bad. So, yes, PTSD does affect my relationship with others - and very negatively.

Similarly, Oscar emphasized that for a while he did not like to socialize much at work:

Me and my peers have a good working relationship now, but before I was very

aloof and didn't talk too much. . . . I would just take care of my patients, go to

lunch when I can, then go home. That wasn't much of a relationship, then but as I

r[o]de through the problem, I became a little more pleasant to be around. I still

didn't tell anyone about my PTSD because I feel it's none of their business, and I

don't want people looking at me weird, like I was incompetent.

Felix noted that he withheld information from colleagues and friends:

Nurses have to have some kind of camaraderie to stay sane in a chaotic world. I

had some buddies I could call loyal friends, but after my deployment . . . it was

hard to function around other nurses, some of whom were my best buddies. I kept

my diagnosis a secret. In nursing or any medical field, we practice patient

privacy. In this case, I was the patient and my diagnosis was not up for

discussion. I lost a few good friends because of my silence about the situation.

Heidi also was not ready to discuss her diagnosis with friends and colleagues:

I'm not ready to open up myself to anyone to talk about PTSD. My friends and

coworkers don't understand what it's like when you hear a sound that reminds

you of the crazy sounds and sirens we used to hear. Environmental stressors like

crowds and things popping and all that is part of my frustration—it's so

frustrating to see myself and compare myself now to what I was before because I

can see the change. Another thing is the medication makes me sleep quite a bit so

I am not good company [*chuckles*].

Cece discussed the difficulty of losing friends because she withdrew socially and did not want to explain why she periodically acted a certain way and why she had become divorced.

We don't really speak anymore because, you know, I ruined those friendships by just withdrawing from them or not going anywhere when they invited me out and just basically, you know, putting them to the side. And no friend—nobody— wants to be friends with somebody who is always grouchy, don't want to go anywhere, always sad and jumpy as heck.

Julia likewise noted that she withheld information and was misleading, which caused relationships to suffer:

The bottom line is that it [PTSD] does affect my relationship with others: my mom, siblings, partners, and even coworkers. I say that because my work life is a façade. I pretend that I am a good, quiet, reserved person at work, but it's really because I don't want anyone to know that sometimes [when] I'm at work I get panic attacks and feel fearful, and I don't want them to know that I sleep around and . . . that I'm afraid of a committed relationship. You know how people are— they are quick to judge you, and who would want to be friends with someone like me?

Olivia described herself as the "biggest liar" because she would hide her feelings and true condition from her husband and friends:

My whole life is, you know, a lie. My husband don't know that I drink a little bit more than, you know, than he does. My friends don't know that either, because most of them drink a glass of wine with us, you know, when they come over, so they don't suspect anything. To me, that's living a lie. I am lying to my husband, lying to my friends, and the worst part is lying to myself. Sometimes when my friends come over, sometimes I just say I'm tired and need to get some rest, because I am too embarrassed to sit there with them knowing that I am not the person they think I am.

In particular, PTSD affected the participants' romantic relationships. Cece perceived that the effects of PTSD, including not wanting to go anywhere, withdrawing emotionally, and being grouchy, contributed to her husband's decision to be unfaithful and, ultimately, to their divorce:

My husband one day finally told me he had cheated on me. . . . The most hurtful part of that was, it was not when I was downrange, not when I was deployed but when I was home, you know, and I guess because I wasn't paying any attention to him, you know. I had no real desire for sex or any intimate stuff like that. Let's just say I was not a participant in it. . . . Looking back now, I seriously wished I never had to deal with PTSD, and that I neglected or refused to take ownership of it before it started to take a toll on my marriage that ended in a divorce.

Viola explained how PTSD decreased the quality of her relationship with her boyfriend. However, unlike Cece and her husband, Viola and her boyfriend remained in their relationship:

I had a companion but no ties. The biggest problem for me is the distance between us emotionally and physically, and it's not for lack of trying—we hardly have any intimacy, and the medications made me gain weight, so that's another part of the intimacy problem, you know what I mean? I have to handle the

127

symptoms of PTSD and trying to look appealing to my boyfriend, and the two . . . don't or just won't work together. He tries very hard to make me feel good about myself in this area, you know, but it is a[n] uphill struggle every day. Then there is the physical exhaustion. It's just too tiring to even try to be intimate—too much work—especially when the depression kicks in.

Luke discussed his occasional urge to leave his fiancée, though his reasons differed from those that ended Cece's marriage and endangered Viola's relationship:

There are days when I feel like just jetting, you know, just leaving so that she wouldn't see me on the bad days when I get jumpy and upset at the most minute things. I tell myself everything is okay because of her and her love and support, but the truth is, I think she deserves better, you know? Someone who is more stable and can give her what she deserves.

Trisha explained that because of PTSD, she was afraid of "getting too close" to others, which led to her having multiple romantic partners. In turn, her promiscuity caused her to withdraw from family members:

I could not keep one partner for too long because as soon as they get close or I feel like I am getting close I pull away. Sometimes I feel like sex helps me to cope better because it takes my mind off things, you know, and is kind of a relief. I feel like that was the only way I could relate to somebody who have no idea what my life was like back then. If I consent to mutual sex, then we both will be happy at least for as long as that lasts. At least I would be worth something to that person, you know, even if it's only for sex. Now you see why I can't talk to my folks, because no one else in the family behaves like this, and I'm sure my

128

mom would say, "I didn't raise you like this, so why all these different partners?" I don't even go home to visit family anymore. I feel like I don't belong there, you know? They are living what I call clean lives, and here I am living a promiscuous life by having all these multiple partners. I'm not sure what the heck I was looking for because, like I said, as soon as there was any sign of closeness, I take off. I guess you could say I felt like a used-up garbage bag that the Army thr[e]w away and no one else was willing to pick me up because nobody wants a bag with holes.

Fear and safety concerns. Four participants (29%) noted that family members and romantic partners felt scared and unsafe around them. The stress and anxiety of having PTSD can sometimes manifest in behaviors that may frighten others. Nightmares and fear are symptoms associated with PTSD. These symptoms may trigger the need to protect self. The soldier may use protective measures, which may cause families and friends to feel unsafe and sometimes withdraw from the soldier. This withdrawal may also intensify the fear and the scenario becomes a cyclic one. For example, Kyle stated the following:

> When I first started having the symptoms, I started putting up burglar bars and cameras and purchased a couple of weapons because I think in the back of my mind I think something bad is going to happen. My wife was concerned about that kind of behavior, you know? She told me when I started doing these things she had concerns of sleeping in our bed. When I heard that, I was devastated. Here I was, inflicting emotional pain on someone that I love.

Luke explained his fiancée felt unsafe around him upon seeing his panic attacks and how he responded:

After I told my fiancée about my diagnosis, she was a little scared, you know, because you hear about the horror stories of soldiers killing themselves or their spouses and even shooting up their buddies on other military installations. So I can't say I really blamed her. . . . I think at first she was scared because I would do crazy things, like jumping out [of] my sleep sweating and breathing real hard. I have to say, that would scare anybody. As much as you try to keep these feelings away from your significant other, the symptoms do manifest in different ways and sometimes can be real scary for others. I have to say, I'm glad she stuck around, because I relied on her for some support and to tell me I wasn't crazy.

Oscar perceived that his entire family suffered. He added that his young child became scared of him because of how he acted: "I was a terrible person at that time. I was mean and constantly yelling at everyone for no good reason, you know? How I could put my family through that is unbelievable when you think of it."

Thematic Summary

Fourteen participants shared their stories of how they were coping and adapting with combat-related PTSD and what that experience has been for them. In their words, stories and non-verbal expressions, themes emerged that presented an insight into the challenges of coping and adapting with PTSD. During each interview, the researcher was present to record the emotional struggles and frustrations shared by the participants. It was apparent to the researcher that the participants all shared a sense of pride in serving

130

their country as a soldier as well as a nurse. For several of the nurses who worked in a civilian environment prior to joining the army, the experience of being an army nurse was different. They saw the experience as one that brought fulfillment to themselves as they provided physical and emotional care to soldiers in a unique environment unlike any other.

On the other side of the pride they shared in serving their country were the challenges of living with PTSD and finding ways to cope with the illness. To provide care in an unpredictable environment as war was evident of the nurses' ability to react quickly and critically think through several options to achieve the positive reward of seeing a soldier return home alive. This act of compassion surpasses their sense of duty. Several nurses had the opportunity to hold a soldier's hand and comfort him or her as they succumb to their wounds and while holding pictures of their families in their hands. All 14 participants shared the common theme of struggling to forget the nightmares of scenarios described above, but they also want to remember the differences they made in the lives of soldiers. From the findings, the emotional struggles and frustration of learning to cope and adapt with PTSD were evident.

Summary

The purpose of this qualitative case study was to explore how veteran army nurses were coping and adapting with combat-related PTSD. After completing a pilot study to evaluate the validity and clarity of the interview questions, 14 participants were interviewed. Each interview was digitally recorded and then transcribed. Analysis of data from the semi-structured interviews was completed with the assistance of NVivo 10 to determine prominent patterns for interpretation. Three themes emerged from data: (1) strategies for coping and adapting, (2) poor self-concept and (3) relationship challenges. The findings presented in Chapter 4 was a representation of the analysis of data gathered from the participants responses provided during interviews. Chapter 5 contains a discussion of the findings, review of the theoretical framework, implications for leadership and nursing, as well as limitations and recommendations for future research.

Chapter 5

Summary, Conclusions and Recommendations

The purpose of this qualitative case study was to explore coping and adaptation in veteran army nurses with combat-related PTSD. Chapter 5 contains discussion on the significance of the research findings. The chapter is organized as follows: (a) summary of findings, (b) comparison of themes with existing literature, (c) connection of themes to the conceptual framework, (d) strengths and limitations, (e) implications of the results followed by a summary.

Statistically, one in every three veterans are diagnosed with PTSD, and less than 40% of them will seek help. On an average, approximately 500 active-duty service members attempt suicide, and 1,100 service members have taken their lives since 2006. Two out of three marriages fail. More than 200,000 military marriages have been broken with 27,000 of that number occurring in 2009 alone (Army Times, 2010). Since the conflicts of the Gulf War and the Global War on Terrorism, there has been an increased focus on PTSD, especially in the military population. A review of the literature revealed research on PTSD in the military in general, as well as PTSD in females specifically, and the issue of PTSD among care givers in the armed forces. However, there were no apparent studies indicating how veteran army nurses were coping and adapting with combat-related PTSD. Three themes emerged from the research data.

Summary of Findings

Each of the three themes that emerged from the research data represented coping and adaptation strategies used by veteran army nurses with combat related PTSD. The themes were: strategies for coping and adapting, poor self-concept and relationship challenges. Theme 1 revealed that participants were demonstrating adaptive and maladaptive behaviors in an effort to cope and adapt. Within this theme, the terms prayer and religion, family and friends, drinking, and avoidance were synonyms that participants used to describe strategies for coping. Coping and adapting included perceptions that prayer and religion were used by religious and nonreligious individuals, and it means something different for everyone. The theme was supported with key words such as "I'm not real big on the religious thing, "pray and meditate," and "yoga and meditation."

Poor self-concept was the second theme of the study. The theme was supported with key words such as "low self-esteem," "loser," and "embarrassment." Some participants defined self-esteem as how they view themselves and not so much of how others view them. This perception required some self-evaluation, which resulted in a negative view of self. Members of stigmatized groups such as those with mental health issues can sometimes have a low concept of self, stemming from societal prejudices as noted in statements such as "I didn't want anyone to know I have PTSD," "I was afraid I would have a hard time finding a job."

The third and final theme, relationship challenges was established as veteran army nurses with combat-related PTSD discussed failures in relationship resulting from having PTSD, and some of the strategies used to cope and adapt. Terms such as "afraid of getting too close," "anger issues," "promiscuity," and "withdrawal" supported this theme.

Though some relationships can survive the strains of PTSD symptoms, others cannot, and sometimes end up in divorce or separation. Anger and guilt are byproducts that can manifest in PTSD. Avoidance, self-blame, low self-esteem, and substance abuse revealed by nurses can also affect intimate and social relationships. Identification of these themes is important because they contain significant connections to the conceptual framework for the study.

Comparison of Themes with Existing Literature

The existing literature regarding coping and adaptation in veteran army nurses with combat-related PTSD was divided into supportive categories with one major category of coping and adaptation. The category of coping and adaptation and the current literature were compared to the three themes revealed by the data. Identification of these themes is significant because it supports the framework for the study and provides a description of how veteran army nurses were coping and adapting with combat-related PTSD. The research findings also demonstrate the gap in the current literature of how these nurses were coping and adapting, as well as how other factors affect PTSD, and how PTSD affect other factors. One supportive category was PTSD and other factors.

PTSD has been shown to influence other areas in individuals' lives and ultimately affect the ability to cope and adapt. The symptoms of PTSD have been shown to intensify and the intensity can be manifested differently for females versus males. Being in a combat environment can be extremely stressful especially for those on the front lines. The same could be said for those who provide medical care, but the evidence for what makes some develop PTSD and others do not, has not been completely definitive. What has been revealed in the literature is that other factors negatively affect symptoms of PTSD, and the intensity of those symptoms determine how a person copes (Bensimon, 2012).

Strategies for Coping and Adaptation

Theme one, strategies for coping and adaptation, described the methods used by veteran army nurses with combat-related PTSD to cope and adapt. One method of coping was prayer and religion. Baljani et al., (2011) found that religion and spiritual well-being are the basis on which individuals build hope. In contrast, Harris et al., (2010) found no substantiating evidence to indicate that prayer helps individuals to overcome traumatic challenges and bring them to a significant level of coping. It has been established that combat exposure is linked with PTSD, and depending on the severity of the exposure, a persons' religious faith can be weakened when he or she finds himself or herself in a situation where he or she is unable to prevent the death and dying often seen in combat (Fontana & Rosenchek, 2004). Individuals use various coping strategies. Some use their religious beliefs, which can be translated as receiving support from God. Others use prayer and reading religious books. Use of these strategies played an important role when attempting to cope with trauma (Freh et al., 2013). Though the participants discussed the importance of religion, meditation, faith and prayer in coping and adapting with PTSD, they did not identify their religious affiliations. From this perspective, one can conclude that the complexities of prayer and religion are not measured by church attendance or religious affiliation, but more of what those concepts mean to individuals.

Another method of coping with combat-related PTSD reportedly used by veteran army nurses was the use of alcohol. Alcohol use seemed to be a common self-medication for PTSD because it dampens the traumatic memory. The Department of Veteran Affairs (VA) (2015) cited that more than 2 of 10 veterans with PTSD also have a diagnosis of substance abuse disorder and 1 in 10 veterans from the Iraq and Afghanistan wars reportedly have problems with alcohol and other drugs. Increased use of alcohol or binge drinking as well as increased avoidance and emotion coping strategies tend to increase PTSD symptoms. A contrasting study revealed that when alcohol is not used for unhealthy reasons, it supposedly lower stress. Also, increased alcohol use was linked to better physical health (Adams et al., 2006). Individuals resiliency and coping strategies also affect the risks of alcohol consumption (Bartone et al., 2012).

Avoidance, which falls into cluster C of the PTSD criteria was another method used by veteran army nurses with combat-related PTSD to cope. The use of behavioral avoidance can sometimes make it difficult for individuals to move on with their lives. The U.S. Department of Veteran Affairs (2015) also cited avoidance as a common response to trauma. Individuals used this emotional avoidance to stop themselves from thinking about the trauma. However, while considered a maladaptive coping measure, avoidance coping may have some merit to it. The VA (2015) posited that avoidance coping may be helpful to some individuals because it helps with the development of other techniques to focus their thoughts and feelings on things that are not related to the trauma. High avoidance coping has been linked to increased chronic PTSD and vice versa (Badour et al., 2012). Avoidance coping was also typically seen in individuals who use alcohol as a form of self-medication.

Poor Self-Concept

Theme two, poor self-concept indicated how veteran army nurses with combat-related PTSD felt about self in relation to PTSD. Self-concept is a combination of beliefs and feelings individuals embrace about themselves, which can vary according to the person. Trauma significantly impacts self-concept, self-image, and self-esteem, and the type of trauma makes no difference in how it affects individuals. Use of avoidance coping can also negatively affect self-concept and the ability to develop love and have compassion for self (Thompson & Waltz, 2008; Slaninova & Stainerova, 2015; Ponsford et al., 2014).

Self-blame was another occurrence within the theme of self-concept. In addressing trauma guilt and PTSD, the National Center for PTSD (2015) reported that more than 40% of people with PTSD report some form of trauma related guilt, which can contribute to development of other psychological problems to include substance abuse. Also, PTSD symptoms are maintained by guilt through a cyclic pattern. Guilt and self-blame thoughts are often seen with traumatic experiences, and these guilt and self-blame thoughts also generates negative emotional responses. This kind of habit causes the traumatic memories to trigger negative emotions that reinforces avoidance which maintains PTSD (National Center for PTSD, 2015). Because poor self-concept and self-esteem are associated with poorer emotional adjustment leading to poorer functional outcomes, it is necessary to address the paradigms of self-concept and self-esteem in individuals, especially those who experienced trauma of some type.

Relationship Challenges

Participants talked about the challenges they experienced with relationships as a result of having PTSD. As previously discussed in this chapter, over 27,000 marriages were broken in 2009 alone. According to Seedat (2012), individuals who are traumatized, especially those with childhood trauma are at increased risks for substance abuse and sexual promiscuity. Tsai et al. (2012), concluded that service members with PTSD reported it was more difficult to maintain their relationships with romantic partners, as well as with family members. In a review of the literature, Galovski and Lyons (2004) reported that combat-related PTSD can "dramatically" impact the families of veterans. The negative behaviors of emotional numbing and withdrawal were cited as also damaging to relationships (Galovski & Lyons, 2004). Fear of spouses and children also emerged from the data. While a natural response when the body is in danger, fear among family members caused by behaviors of the veterans, can be frightening. Family members sometime become fearful when they see their loved ones demonstrating symptoms contrary to who the individual was before deployment. Interestingly, in the instances where fear was reported, none of those relationships ended in divorce or separation.

Connection to the Conceptual Framework

The conceptual framework for the study was Roy Adaptation Model. Assumptions of the model are that individuals are bio-psycho-social beings who are constantly interacting with a changing environment. The individual uses both innate and acquired strategies to cope with environmental changes. The individual's behavior in response to coping and adaptation can be observed in 4 adaptive modes which are:

139

physiological, self-concept, role function, and interdependence (Roy, 2009). While all modes are relevant, the research study focused on coping and adaptation using the self-concept, role function, and interdependence modes. Within the 4 modes of adaptation are 3 adaptation levels categorized as integrated, compensatory, and compromised. Comparing the research data with the modes and levels of adaptation was useful in understanding the connections between the conceptual framework and how veteran army nurses cope and adapt with combat-related PTSD.

Effective coping and adaptation is the extent to which an individual is able to effectively meet the demands identified in each adaptive mode thereby placing that individual at an integrated coping and adaptation level. Data from the research indicated that veteran army nurses with combat-related PTSD in the study were at the compensatory coping and adaptation level. The nursing process according to the RAM begins with the assessment of behavior within the 4 adaptive modes. The assessment includes gathering behavioral data and tentatively judging that behavior (Roy, 2009). While this approach is possible with the individual assessment, in the case of a group such as veteran army nurses with combat-related PTSD, when data reveals the interactions of individuals within that group the RAM concept also provides for coping and adaptation levels to indicate how well the group is engaged in meeting the needs of the 4 modes. Therefore, coping and adaptation levels are derived from an assessment of the adaptive modes. In this study, the data provided sufficient details to convey a coping and adaptation level for each participant because they described the extent to which needs within the 3 adaptive modes were met.

Self-Concept Mode

The self-concept mode is how an individual sees himself or herself. It is divided into two subareas: the physical self and the personal self, which includes body image and body sensation. Body image is an individual's mental image of his or her body; body sensation is a combination of the individual's values and feelings (Roy, 2009). Data from the study indicated that participants had a poor concept of self with low self-esteem, feelings of worthlessness, and self-blame, all from which the theme of low self-concept emerged. Participants described how they felt about themselves having combat-related PTSD, and how they perceived others saw them. The research described how various traumas affected a persons' self-concept. The adaptive problems identified in the study were loss of self and relationships, and low self-esteem. Themes 2 and 3 emerged from the data as participants described their concept of self, and in relation to others. The responses provided information that covered the 3 modes of focus in the study, providing support for the interrelationship between the modes of RAM.

Role Function Mode

The role-function mode refers to the individual's societal role based on his or her position within society (Roy, 2009). Some participants reported not being able to fully function in their spousal role, or not being able to work as a nurse as they described the impact of combat-related PTSD. Others described the inability to work for fear of emotional reactions toward others. There were instances where children voiced their concerns and even demonstrated fear in response to how the veteran assumed his or her parental role. The research data demonstrated the impact of combat-related PTSD on the veteran and his or her societal roles. The effects sometimes led veterans to substance

141

abuse as a coping measure. Displacement of the veteran's societal roles contributed to low self-concept and low self-esteem. The adaptive problem identified in the study was a lack of social integrity.

Interdependence Mode

Close intimate relationships with significant others, being valued, and respected are the focuses of the interdependence mode (Roy, 2009). The adaptive problems identified in the study were a lack of relational integrity, low self-value, and insecurity in nurturing relationships. While participants implicitly revealed some stable family relationships, others reported withdrawal from friends and families. They also described feelings of worthlessness to themselves, families, and society. Research showed that service members with PTSD reported more difficulties in maintaining intimate and familial relationships.

Coping and Adaptation Levels

As discussed, within the 4 modes of RAM are 3 levels of coping and adaptation that would indicate the effectiveness of an individual's coping processes and adaptive behaviors: integrated, compensatory, and compromised. Each level is the degree to which a person successfully meets the needs identified in that adaptive mode. The emerging themes from the data analysis revealed that while participants were not at the integrated compensatory level, they were using some strategies to assist with coping. This approach places them at the compensatory adaptation level.

Integrated adaptation level. The human system functioning at the integrated level is an indication that the individual is fully functioning as a whole to meet the human needs. The process could be described as the individual effectively coping in all 4 modes of the RAM. Based on the coping strategies participants used in response to the focal and contextual stimuli, the data did not reveal that they were at the integrated adaptation level.

Compensatory adaptation level. Individuals are sometimes engaged in compensatory coping where demands are recognized and determined to exceed present capabilities. Participants in the study recognized the demands (PTSD symptoms, flashbacks and other contextual factors) as well as the negative impact on self and family if they allow the demands to exceed their coping capacity. To respond to the demands of PTSD, participants compensated by creating alternate pathways and employed other resources in an effort to reach the integrated level of coping. At the time of the research, when data was categorized and viewed from within the 3 modes of the RAM (Figure 6), which was the focus of the study, the results indicated that participants were at the compensatory adaptation level. Participants employed sufficient coping strategies such as prayer and religion, support systems, medications and therapy, as well as other resources to compensate in each of the 3 modes.

Compromised adaptation level. Individuals at this level are demonstrating ineffective coping and adaptation approaches. The compensatory and integrated processes are employed in the human system, but are ineffective in fully managing the challenge. When responding to the challenge exceeds the individual's coping capacity and additional resources are ineffective, the area of functioning is considered

143

compromised (Roy, 2009). In the study, participants discussed the strategies they used

for coping, indicating that they were able to manage the challenges in some areas by

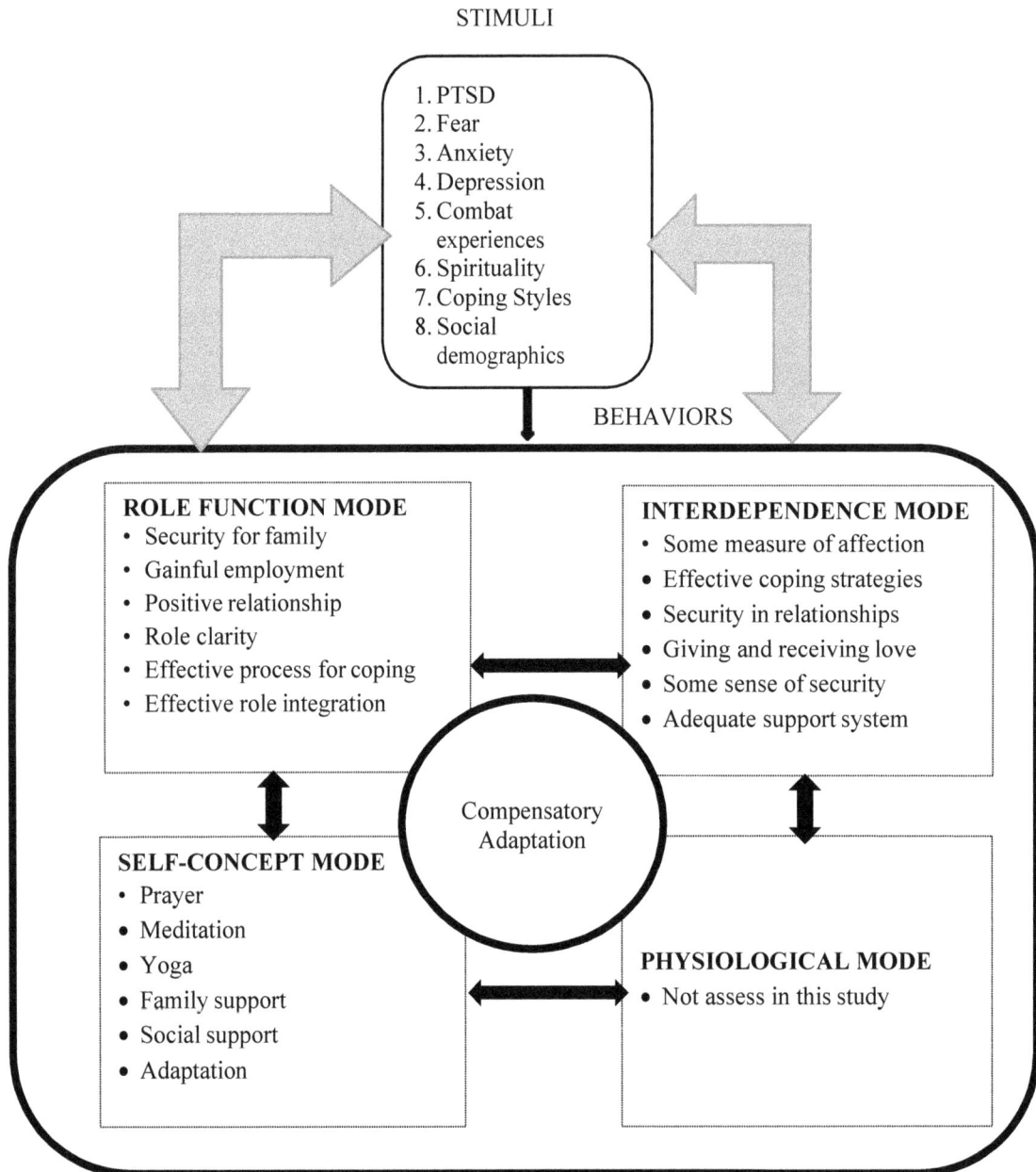

compensating.

STIMULI

1. PTSD
2. Fear
3. Anxiety
4. Depression
5. Combat experiences
6. Spirituality
7. Coping Styles
8. Social demographics

BEHAVIORS

ROLE FUNCTION MODE
- Security for family
- Gainful employment
- Positive relationship
- Role clarity
- Effective process for coping
- Effective role integration

INTERDEPENDENCE MODE
- Some measure of affection
- Effective coping strategies
- Security in relationships
- Giving and receiving love
- Some sense of security
- Adequate support system

Compensatory Adaptation

SELF-CONCEPT MODE
- Prayer
- Meditation
- Yoga
- Family support
- Social support
- Adaptation

PHYSIOLOGICAL MODE
- Not assess in this study

Figure 6. Themes in relation to RAM.

144

Strengths and Limitations

Strengths of the research study were demonstrated through the research participants as well as the interview process. Data emerged through the interview process to answer the research questions. A limitation of the study was the location of the research, which was confined to one area around a military base. A strength of the study was in the research interviews. After data saturation was identified, interviews continued and each transcript was reviewed several times to determine any new themes. Also, participants were given the opportunity to review their responses for clarification.

Another limitation of the study was the sample size of 14 participants, which made it difficult to generalize as the sample was not an adequate representation of the population. Another strength of the study was with the research participants. The participants were both males and females from different ethnicity and culture, and had deployment experiences that were unique to each of them. Therefore, they were able to provide the rich data needed in answer to the research questions. Researcher bias was another limitation because the researcher was a registered nurse who had been deployed in support of one of the three conflicts, and who also had a diagnosis of combat-related PTSD. The narrowed focus on coping and adaptation from the perspective of a specific group of army nurses was also a limitation of the study.

Recommendations

The results of the study showed that veteran army nurses with combat-related PTSD were employing different resources to assist them in coping with the demands of illness. From the perspective of the RAM, these nurses were using compensatory coping processes. The goal is to assist them to reach the integrated coping process where they are able to use all available resources to help them function effectively.

Currently, a significant amount of programs are available to veterans through the VA. However, because no literature was found on the coping and adaptation of veteran army nurses with combat-related PTSD, more efforts are needed to determine if any, and what resources are available to these nurses that would provide them with the strategies they need to effectively cope and adapt with combat-related PTSD. The efforts to address the needs of the veteran must continue, especially in the VA as more veterans are returning from the Global War on Terrorism with PTSD and traumatic brain injuries. Several recommendations are discussed. The current focus on PTSD should extend beyond treatments for symptomatic relief to a focus of addressing the coping and adaptation needs of veteran army nurses with combat-related PTSD. The role of nurses in a combat environment is critical to the survival of the men and women they support in and out of that environment, which ultimately extends to the survival of the nation. Policy makers within the Army Nurse Corps, the Army Medical Command, the VA, nursing educators and others in the military community are all in positions to influence significant changes to benefit veteran army nurses with combat-related PTSD and their families. The first step is to cultivate awareness of how these nurses are coping. An army-wide survey of veteran army nurses with combat-related PTSD could generate data that would promote this awareness. Secondly, the VA and the Army Medical Department should extend assistance within their power of influence, which will either directly assist or lead to research, policies, or nursing interventions that may improve coping and adaptation strategies for this group of nurses. Finally, The VA currently uses an online system where veterans can access personal health care information. Extending this system to incorporate regular assessment of this specific group of veterans by using a checklist specifically targeting coping and adaptation could generate information that would help determine if the veteran army nurse is functioning as a human adaptive system when confronted with the stress of combat-related PTSD.

Implications

The findings of this qualitative, single case-study supports the basic concepts of the Roy Adaptation Model, which theorized that the human system is an adaptive one that is constantly influenced by stimuli. The focal, contextual, and residual stimuli are processed through the four adaptive modes resulting in behavior. Assessment of behavior determines the adaptive level of the person, namely integrated, compensatory, and compromised adaptation (Roy, 2009). The focus of the study was to explore how veteran army nurses with combat-related PTSD were coping and adapting when confronted with the stress of PTSD. The RAM was used as a theoretical framework to guide this focus. A tenet of the RAM theorized that the four adaptive modes are interrelated and overlap. Therefore, one mode can compensate for ineffective coping in another mode as seen in the study results (Roy, 2009).

Implications for Nursing

Nurses strive to promote holistic health and wellness to the human system through caring, oftentimes giving little attention to themselves. Sometimes these actions can lead to burn-out, and frustration if adequate coping strategies are not used. One purpose of research is to extend knowledge. It is important that nurses understand that as adaptive systems, people respond within their various life situations. To reach this level of understanding requires nurses to first understand their own values, beliefs, and emotions. Having this understanding of self could contribute to understanding the human system as a sum of all its parts. This knowledge would result in the possible development of appropriate nursing interventions to support caring from a holistic perspective.

Implications for Leadership

People choose to join the Army for various reasons. The implied understanding is at some point an individual may deploy to a combat area. The physical and mental consequences of deployment are unpredictable. How a person copes and adapts to the consequences differs because as demonstrated in the research, people respond differently to the focal, contextual, and residual stimuli in their environment. Results of this study indicated that the veteran nurses were using compensatory coping to create a balance in their lives. Some individuals spoke about feeling worthless and useless because they were not able to function in their role anymore. Most of the participants were retired either medically or otherwise. The milieu of the Army is one that is comparable to a family. When individuals can no longer function in their role within the family, they may feel some kind of value if they are embraced by the family, instead of focusing on the inability to function in that specific role. More efforts could be made to reach out to these nurses and their families either through the media or targeted events for the veteran nurse.

Implications for Research

Roy's Adaptation Model has been used in various researches over the years to explore the concepts of coping and adaptation in several areas. In this research study, the model proved to be useful when assessing participants' coping and adaptation level within the constraints of the RAM. Based on the literature, the concept of coping is fluid. An understanding and application of the philosophical assumptions of the RAM provide a basis for assessing coping and adaptation in the veteran army nurse.

In the study a qualitative approach was used to explore coping and adaption of veteran army nurses with combat-related PTSD. The study should be replicated using a quantitative approach, a larger group of nurses, nurses from all branches of the military, and a broader geographic scope. A quantitative approach could use measures that would not require participants to interact face-to-face with the researcher. Eliminating this factor might lead to participants revealing more information.

Future nursing research is indicated on what coping strategies, if any, nurses use upon returning home and possibly while in the combat environment. Based on the RAM, it is ideal for individuals to operate at the integrated level. As mentioned, participants in this study were using compensatory processes. Participants also used a combination of emotion-focus coping, problem-solving coping and approached-based coping. Future nursing research directions could focus on coping in these specific areas, especially approached-based coping in veteran army nurses with combat-related PTSD.

Conclusions

Three themes emerged from the data generated in this qualitative single case-study on coping and adaptation of veteran army nurses with combat-related PTSD. Analysis of the data suggested this group of nurses were not functioning as a human adaptive system at the integrated level, but that they developed pathways to compensate using other contextual resources. The theoretical framework of Roy Adaptation Model was used to generate three research questions that guided the interview process. Data were analyzed with content analysis using the deductive approach.

These findings, supported by the research, prompted recommendations for improved processes, policies, and resources specifically for the targeted population. If implemented successfully, the results would be beneficial not only for veteran army nurses with combat-related PTSD, but for veteran nurses with combat-related PTSD in other branches of the military. While some effective coping strategies emerged from the data, others such as avoidance coping and the use of alcohol were considered maladaptive behaviors. PTSD is a global illness affecting individuals and families in various ways and can sometimes be debilitating. In the US, approximately 22 veterans died from suicide each day in 2010 (VA, 2012). Since then, thousands of veterans returned from Iraq and Afghanistan with PTSD, which is usually an underlying factor for suicide. When faced with the stress of PTSD, it is vital for individuals to have and employ effecting coping and adaptation strategies to function at the ideal integrated level, or at least be able to compensate to manage the impact of the illness. As research continues on the issue of PTSD and its impact on the lives of individuals, families, and society, it is critical to focus on coping and adaptation skills of individuals affected by this illness.

References

9/11: Ten years on. (2011). The Lancet, 378(9794), 849. Retrieved from

    http://www.thelancet.com

Adams, R. E., Boscarino, J. A., & Galea, S. (2006). Alcohol use, mental health status and

    psychological well-being 2 years after the world trade center attacks in New York

    City. *American Journal of Drug & Alcohol Abuse, 32*(2), 203-224.doi:

    10.1080/00952990500479522

Afrasiabifar, A., Karimi, Z., & Hassani, P. (2013). Roy's adaptation model-based patient

    education for promoting the adaptation of hemodialysis patients. *Iranian Red*

    Crescent Medical Journal, 15(7), 566-572. doi:10.5812/ircmj.12024

Ahmadi, N., Hajsadeghi, F., Mirshkarlo, H. B., Budoff, M., Yehuda, R., & Ebrahimi, R.

    (2011). Post-traumatic stress disorder, coronary atherosclerosis, and mortality.

    American Journal of Cardiology, 108(1), 29-33.

    doi:10.1016/j.amjcard.2011.02.340

Aldwin, C. M. (2007). *Stress, coping, and development: An integrative perspective* (2nd

    ed.). New York, NY: Guilford Press.

American Psychiatric Association. (2000). *Diagnostic and statistical manual of mental*

    disorders (4th ed.). Washington, DC: Author.

American Psychiatric Association. (2013). *Diagnostic and statistical manual of mental*

    disorders (5th ed.). Washington, DC: Author.

Angelou, M. (1978). *And still I rise.* New York, NY: Random House.

Antai-Otong, D. (2008). *Psychiatric nursing: Biological and behavioral concepts* (2nd

    ed.). Clifton Park, NY: Thomson/Delmar Learning.

Army Medical Department. (2014). *Army Nurse Corps history*. Retrieved from

http://history.amedd.army.mil/ANCWebsite/anchome.html.

Badour, C. L., Blonigen, D. M., Boden, M. T., Feldner, M. T., & Bonn-Miller, M. O.

(2012). A longitudinal test of the bi-directional relations between avoidance

coping and PTSD severity during and after PTSD treatment. *Behaviour Research*

and Therapy, *50*(10), 610–616. doi:10.1016/j.brat.2012.06.006

Baljani, E., Khashabi, J., Amanpour, E., & Azimi, N. (2011). Relationship between

spiritual well-being, religion, and hope among patients with cancer. *Hayati*

Journal of Biosciences, *17*(3), 27–37. Retrieved from

http://web.b.ebscohost.com.contentproxy.phoenix.edu

Banner, D., & Zimmer, L. (2012). Informed consent in research: An overview for nurses.

Canadian Journal Of Cardiovascular Nursing, *22*(1), 26-30 5p. Retrieved from

http://web.b.ebscohost.com.contentproxy.phoenix.edu

Bartone, P. T., Hystad, S.W., Eid, J., & Brevik, J. I. (2012). Psychological hardiness and

coping style as risk/resilience factors for alcohol abuse. *Military Medicine,*

177(5), 517-24. doi:10.7205/MILMED-D-11-00200

Baxter, P., & Jack, S. (2008). Qualitative case study methodology: Study design and

implementation for novice researchers. *The Qualitative Report, 13*(4), 544–559.

Retrieved from http://www.nova.edu/ssss/QR/

Bensimon, M. (2012). Elaboration on the association between trauma, PTSD and

posttraumatic growth: The role of trait resilience. *Personality and Individual*

Differences, *52*(7), 782–787. Doi:10.1016/j.paid.2012.01.011

Bentley, S. (2005). *Vietnam Veterans of America: The Veteran.* Retrieved from

http://www.vva.org/archive/TheVeteran/2005_03/feature_HistoryPTSD.htm

Berg, B. L. (2008). *Qualitative research methods for the social sciences* (7th ed.).

Boston, MA: Allyn & Bacon.

Bhutto, Z. H., & Imtiaz, S. (2011). Differences of coping responses between genders.

Pakistan Journal of Clinical Psychology, (1), 29-41.

doi:10.1080/00313830701485460

Boivin, J. (2005). New generation of Army nurses won't suffer PTSD under general's

watch. Retrieved from http://news.nurse.com/article/20050328/PA/503280367

Boscarino, J. A. (2008). A prospective study of PTSD and early-age heart disease

mortality among Vietnam veterans: Implications for surveillance and prevention.

Psychosomatic Medicine, 70(6), 668–676. doi:10.1097/PSY.0b013e31817bccaf

Brodsky, A. (2008). Researcher as instrument. In L. Given (Ed.), *The SAGE encyclopedia

of qualitative research methods.* (pp. 767-768). Thousand Oaks, CA: Sage

Publications.

Charmaz, K. (2006). *Constructing grounded theory: A practical guide through

qualitative analysis.* Thousand Oaks, CA: Sage Publications.

Chenail, R. J. (2011). Interviewing the investigator: Strategies for addressing

instrumentation and researcher bias concerns in qualitative research. *The

Qualitative Report, 16*(1), 255-262. http://search.proquest.com./docview/

Conard, P. L., & Sauls, D. J. (2014). Deployment and PTSD in the female combat

veteran: a systematic review. *Nursing Forum, 49*(1), 1-10. Doi:10.1111/nuf.12049

153

Conard, P. L., Young, C., Hogan, L., & Armstrong, M. L. (2014). Encountering women veterans with military sexual trauma. *Perspectives in Psychiatric Care, 50,* 1-7. doi:10.1111/ppc.12055

Corbin, J., & Strauss, A. (2015). *Basics of Qualitative Research. Techniques and Procedures for Developing Grounded Theory* (4th ed.). Thousand Oaks: CA: Sage Publications.

Coyne, I. T. (2008). Sampling in qualitative research. Purposeful and theoretical sampling; merging or clear boundaries? *Journal of Advance Nursing, 26*(3), 623-630. doi:10.1046/j.1365-2648.1997.t01-25-00999

Crain, J. A., Larson, G. E., Highfill-McRoy, R. M. & Schmied, E.A. (2011). Postcombat outcomes among Marines with preexisting mental diagnoses. *Journal of Trauma Stress, 24*(6), 671-679. doi: 10.1002/jts.20700

Crotty, M. (1998). *The foundations of social research: Meaning and perspective in the research process.* Thousand Oaks, CA: Sage Publications.

Cypress, B. S. (2011). Patient-family-nurse intensive care unit experience: A Roy adaptation model-based qualitative study. *Qualitative Research Journal (RMIT Training Pty Ltd Trading As RMIT Publishing), 11*(2), 3-16. doi:10.3316/QRJ1102003

Defense Casualty Analysis System. (2013). *Timeline view.* Retrieved from https://www.dmdc.osd.mil/dcas/pages/timeline.xhtml

Defense Manpower Data Center. (2013). *Army Nurse Corps fiscal years deployment data.* Retrieved from https://www.dmdc.osd.mil

Delva, M. D., Kirby, J. R., Knapper, C. K. & Birtwhistle, R. V. (2002). Postal survey of

approaches to learning among Ontario physicians: Implications for continuing

medical education. *British Medical Journal, 325*(7374), 1218-1220.

doi:10.1136/bmj.325.7374.1218

Denzin, N. K., & Lincoln, Y. S. (2008). (Eds.). *The landscape of qualitative research*

(3rd ed.). Los Angeles, CA: Sage Publications.

Department of Defense. Military Casualty Information Web site. 2007. As of January 3,

2008: http://siadapp.dmdc.osd.mil/personnel/CASUALTY/castop.htm

Department of Veteran Affairs (2014). *Suicide Data Report*. Retrieved from

http://www.va.gov/opa/docs/Suicide-Data-Report-2012-final.pdf

Department of Veteran Affairs (2015). *PTSD and substance abuse*. Retrieved from

http://www.ptsd.va.gov/public/problems/ptsd_substance_abuse_veterans.asp

Deployment Health and Family Readiness Library. (2006). *New emotional cycles of*

deployment for service members and their families. Retrieved from

http://deploymenthealthlibrary.fhp.osd.mil

Devers, K. J., & Frankel, R. M. (2000). Study design in qualitative research: Sampling

and data collection strategies. *Education for Health, 13*(2), 263–271.

doi:10.1080/13576280050074543

Dickson-Swift, V., James, E. L., Kippen, S., & Liamputtong, P. (2009). Researching

sensitive topics: qualitative research as emotion work. *Qualitative Research, 9*(1),

61-79. doi:10.1002/jts.20163

155

Doolittle, B., Courtney, M., & Jasien, J. (2015). Satisfaction with life, coping, and

    spirituality among urban families. *Journal of Primary Care & Community Health,*

    6 (4), 256-259. doi:10.1177/2150131915596961

Eight years of war take toll on military marriages. (2010). *Army Times.* Retrieved from

    http://archive.armytimes.com/article/20100217/

Elo, S., & Kyngäs, H. (2007) The qualitative content analysis process. *Journal of*

    Advanced Nursing 62(1), 107-115. doi:10.1111/j.1365-2648.2007.04569.x

Epidemiology program, post-deployment health group, office of public health, veterans

    health administration, department of veterans affairs. (2014). *Analysis of VA*

    health care utilization among operation enduring freedom, operation Iraqi

    freedom, and operation new dawn veterans, from 1st Qtr FY 2002 through 4th

    Qtr FY 2014. Washington, DC: Author. Retrieved from

    http://www.publichealth.va.gov/epidemiology

Feczer, D., & Bjorklund, P. (2009). Forever changed: Posttraumatic stress disorder in

    female military veterans, a case report. *Perspectives in Psychiatric Care, 45*(4),

    278-291. doi:10.1111/j.1744-6163.2009.00230.x

Feller, C. M., & Moore, C. J. (Eds.). (1995). *Highlights in the history of the Army Nurse*

    Corps. United States Army Center of Military History. Washington, DC.

    Retrieved from http://www.history.army.mil/html/

Fontana, A., & Rosencheck R. (2004). Trauma, change in strength of religious faith, and

    mental health service use among veterans treated for PTSD. *Journal of Nervous*

    and Mental Disease, 192(9), 579–584.

    doi:10.1097/01.nmd.0000138224.17375.55

Freh, F. M., Dallos, R., & Chung, M. C. (2013). An exploration of PTSD and coping strategies: Response to the experience of being in a bomb attack in Iraq. *Traumatology: An International Journal, 19*(2), 87-94. doi:10.1177/1534765612444882

Friedman, M. J., Keane, T. M, & Resick, P. A. (Eds.). (2010). *Handbook of PTSD: Science and practice*. New York, NY: Guilford.

Frydenberg, E. (2002). *Beyond coping: Meeting goals, visions, and challenges*. New York, NY: Oxford University Press.

Fusch, P. I., & Ness, L. R. (2015). Are we there yet? Data saturation in qualitative research. *Qualitative Report, 20*(9), 1408–1416. Retrieved from http://www.nova.edu

Gagliardi, B. A., Frederickson, K., & Shanley, D. A. (2002). Living with multiple sclerosis: a Roy adaptation model-based study. *Nursing Science Quarterly Living, 15*(3), 230-236. doi:10.1177/08918402015003009

Galovski, T., & Lyons, J. A. (2004). Psychological sequelae of combat violence: A review of the impact of PTSD on the veteran's family and possible interventions. *Aggression and Violent Behavior, 9*(5), 477-501. doi:10.1016/S1359-1789(03)00045-4

Ghafoori, B., Barragan, B., Tohidian, N., & Palinkas, L. (2012). Racial and ethnic differences in symptom severity of PTSD, GAD, and depression in trauma-exposed, urban, treatment-seeking adults. *Journal of Traumatic Stress, 25*(1), 106-110. doi:10.1002/jts.21663

Gibbons, S. W., Barnett, S. D., M., Hickling, E. J., & Herbig-Wall, P. L. (2012). Stress, coping, and mental health-seeking behaviors: Gender differences in OEF/OIF health care providers. *Journal of Traumatic Stress 25*, 115-119. doi: 10.1002/jts.21661.

Gradus, J. L. (2015). *Epidemiology of PTSD*. Retrieved from ptsd.va.gov/professional/PTSD-overview/

Graneheim, U. H., & Lundman, B. (2004). Qualitative content analysis in nursing research: Concepts, procedures and measures to achieve trustworthiness. *Nurse Education Today, 4*(2), 105-112. doi:10.1016/j.nedt.2003.10.001

Hancock, D. R. & Algozzine, B. (2011). *Doing case study research: A practical guide for beginning researchers*. (2nd ed.). New York, NY: Teachers College Press.

Harris, J. I., Erbes, C. R., Engdahl, B. E., Tedeschi, R. G., Olson, R. H., Marie, A., … Mcmahill, J. (2010). Coping functions of prayer and posttraumatic growth. *The International Journal for the Psychology of Religion, 20,* 26-38. doi: 10.1080/10508610903418103

Higginbottom, G. M. A. (2004). Sampling issues in qualitative research. *Nurse Researcher, 12*(1), 7-19. doi:10.7748/nr2004.07.12.1.7.c5927

Himmelfarb, N., Yaeger, D., & Mintz, L. (2006). Posttraumatic stress disorder in female veterans with military and civilian sexual. *Journal of Trauma Stress*, 19(6), 837-846. doi:10.1002/jts.20163

Hoe, J., & Hoare, Z. (2013). Understanding quantitative research: Part 1. *Nursing Standard, 27*(15-17), 52-7; quiz 58. Retrieved from http://search.proquest.com/docview/

Hoge, C. W., & Castro, C. A. (2005). *Impact of combat duty in Iraq and Afghanistan on the mental health of U.S. soldiers: Findings from the Walter Reed Army Institute of Research Land Combat Study.* In NATO Science and Technology Organization (Ed.), Strategies to maintain combat readiness during extended deployments: A human systems approach (pp. 11.1–11.6). Retrieved from http://www.rto.nato.int/abstracts.asp

Hoge, C. W., Auchterlonie, J. L., & Milliken, C. S. (2006). Mental health problems, use of mental health services, and attrition from military service after returning from deployment to Iraq or Afghanistan. *Journal of the American Medical Association, 295*(9), 1023–1032. doi:10.1001/jama.295.9.1023

Houghton, C., Casey, D., Shaw, D., & Murphy, K. (2013). Rigor in qualitative case-study research. *Nurse Researcher, 20*(4), 12-17. doi:10.7748/nr2013.03.20.4.12.e326

Hsieh, H.-F., & Shannon, S. E. (2005). Three approaches to qualitative content analysis. *Qualitative Health Research, 15*(9), 1277-1288. doi:10.1177/1049732305276687

Idsoe, T., Dyregrov, A., & Idsoe, E. C. (2012). Bullying and PTSD symptoms. *Journal of Abnormal Child Psychology, 40*(6), 901-911. doi:10.1007/s10802-012-9620-0

Isbir, G., & Mete, S. (2013). Experiences with nausea and vomiting during pregnancy in Turkish women based on Roy adaptation model: A content analysis. *Asian Nursing Research, 7*(4), 175-181. doi:10.1016/j.anr.2013.09.006

James, D. L. (2013) *Case study: Succession planning in a nonprofit organization* (Doctoral dissertation). Retrieved from ProQuest Dissertations and Theses database. (UMI No. 3570572).

Jensen, D. (2008). *Dependability*. In L. Given (Ed.), The Sage encyclopedia of qualitative research methods. (pp. 209-210). Thousand Oaks, CA: Sage Publications. doi:10.4135/9781412963909.n106

Jones, E. (2011). The military and its psychiatric challenges. *International Review of Psychiatry, 23*(2), 125-126. doi:10.3109/09540261.2011.562010

Kang, H. K., Natelson, B. H., Mahan, C. M., Lee, K. Y., & Murphy, F. M. (2003). Post-traumatic stress disorder and chronic fatigue syndrome-like illness among Gulf War veterans: A population-based survey of 30,000 Veterans. *American Journal of Epidemiology*, 157(2):141-148. doi:/10.1093/aje/kwf187

Kaiser, A. P., Spiro, A., III, Lee, L. O., & Stellman, J. M. (2012). Women Vietnam veterans: Do PTSD symptoms mediate effects of warzone service on health? *Research in Human Development, 9*(3), 210-228. doi:10.1080/15427609.2012.705553

Kelly, U.A., Skelton, K., Patel, M., & Bradley, B. (2011). More than military sexual trauma: Interpersonal violence, PTSD, and mental health in women veterans. *Research in Nursing and Health, 34*(6), 457-467. doi.org/10.1002/nur.20453

Kessler, R. C., Sonnega, A., Bromet, E., Hughes, M., & Nelson, C. B. (1995). Posttraumatic stress disorder in the national comorbidity survey. *Archives of General Psychiatry, 52,* 1048-1060. doi:10.1001/archpsyc.1995.03950240066012

Kimerling, R., Gima, K., Smith, M. W., Street, A., & Frayne, S. (2007). The Veterans Health Administration and military sexual trauma. *American Journal of Public Health, 97*(12), 2160–2166. doi:10.2105/AJPH.2006.092999.

160

King, L. A., King, D. W., Vogt, D. S., Knight, J., & Samper, R. E. (2006). Deployment risk and resilience inventory: A collection of measures for studying deployment-related experiences of military personnel and veteran. *Military Psychology, 18*(2), 89-120. doi:10.1207/s15327876mp1802_1

Koenen, K. C., Stellman, S. D., Sommer, J. F., Jr., & Stellman, J. M. (2008). Persisting posttraumatic stress disorder symptoms and their relationship to functioning in Vietnam veterans: A 14-year follow-up. *Journal of Traumatic Stress, 21*(1), 49-57. doi:10.1002/jts.20304

Kondracki, N. L., Wellman, N. S., & Amundson, D. R. (2002). Content analysis: Review of methods and their applications in nutrition education. *Journal of Nutrition Education and Behavior, 34*(4), 224-230. doi:10.1016/S1499-4046(06)60097-3

Kulka, R. A., Schlenger, W. A., Fairbank, J. A., Hough, R. L., Jordan, B. K., Marmar, C. R., & Weiss, D. S. (1988). *Contractual report of findings from the National Vietnam Veterans readjustment study* (Vols. 1-4). Research Triangle Institute. Retrieved from http://www.ptsd.va.gov/professional/research-bio/research

Kulka, R. A., Schlenger, W. A., Fairbanks, J.A., Hough, R.L., Jordan, B. K., Marmar, C.R., ... Cranston, A.S. (1990). *Trauma and the Vietnam War generation: Report of findings from the National Vietnam Veterans Readjustment Study*. New York: Brunner/Mazel.

Kvale, S., & Brinkmann, S. (2009). *Interviews: Learning the craft of qualitative research interviewing* (2nd ed.). Los Angeles, CA: Sage Publications.

Lazarus, R. S. (1991). *Emotion and adaptation*. New York, NY: Oxford University Press.

Lazarus, R. S. (1993). Coping theory and research: Past, present and future. *Psychosomatic Medicine, 55*, 234-247. doi:10.1097/00006842-199305000-00002

Lazarus, R. S. (1999). *Stress and emotion: A new synthesis.* New York, NY: Springer.

LeBlanc, V. R., Regehr, C., Jelley, R. B., & Barath, I. (2007). Does posttraumatic stress disorder (PTSD) affect performance? *Journal of Nervous and Mental Disease, 195*(8), 701-704. doi:10.1097/NMD.0b013e31811f4481

Li, H. J., & Shyu, Y. I. L. (2007). Coping processes of Taiwanese families during the postdischarge period for an elderly family member with hip fracture. *Nursing Science Quarterly, 20*(3), 273-279. doi:10.1177/0894318407303128

Lincoln, Y. S., & Guba, E. G. (1990). *Naturalistic Inquiry.* Beverly Hills, CA: Sage Publications.

Looper, R. R. (2012). *Adaptation and coping processes as reported by army reservists and their families throughout one year following the soldier's deployment to combat locations* (Doctoral dissertation). Retrieved from Proquest Dissertations & Theses Full Text. (Order No. 3547248).

Marine Corps Times (2010). *8 years of war take toll on military marriages.* Retrieved from http://archive.marinecorpstimes.com/article/20100217

Martz, E., Bodner, T., & Livneh, H. (2009). Coping as a moderator of disability and psychosocial adaptation among Vietnam theater veterans. *Journal of Clinical Psychology, 65*(1), 94-112. doi:10.1002/jclp.20541

Mason, M. (2010). Sample size and saturation in PhD studies using qualitative interviews. *Forum: Qualitative Social Research 11*(3). Retrieved from http://search.proquest.com.contentproxy.phoenix.edu

162

Mayring, P. (2000). Qualitative content analysis. *Forum: Qualitative Social Research, 1*(2), 1-10. Retrieved from http://search.proquest.com.contentproxy.phoenix.edu

McDonald, A., Danielson, C. K., Resnick, H. S., Saunders, B. E., & Kilpatrick, D. G. (2010). PTSD and comorbid disorders in a representative sample of adolescents: The risk associated with multiple exposures to potentially traumatic events. *Child Abuse and Neglect, 34*(10), 773-783. doi:10.1016/j.chiabu.2010.03.006

Mealer, M., Jones, J., & Moss, M. (2012). A qualitative study of resilience and posttraumatic stress disorder in united states ICU nurses. *Intensive Care Medicine, 38*(9), 1445-1451. doi10.1007/s00134-012-2600-6

Meffert, S. M., Metzler, T. J., Henn-Haase, C., McCaslin, S., Inslicht, S., Chemtob, C., … Marmar, C. R. (2008). A prospective study of trait anger and PTSD symptoms in police. *Journal Of Traumatic Stress, 21*(4), 410-416. doi:10.1002/jts.20350

Meis, L. A., Erbes, C. R., Polusny, M. A., & Compton, J. S. (2010). Intimate relationships among returning soldiers: the mediating and moderating roles of negative emotionality, PTSD symptoms, and alcohol problems. *Journal Of Traumatic Stress, 23*(5), 564-572. doi:10.1002/jts.20560

Merriam, S. B. (2009). *Qualitative research: A guide to design and implementation* (2nd ed.). San Francisco, CA: Josey-Bass.

Miller, M. W., Kaloupek, D. G., Dillon, A. L., & Keane, T. M. (2004). Externalizing and internalizing subtypes of combat-related PTSD: A replication and extension using the PSY-5 scales. *Journal of Abnormal Psychology, 113*(4), 636-645. doi:10.1037/0021-843X.113.4.636

Monahan, E., & Neidel-Greenlee, R., (2004). And if I perish: Nurse leadership in World War II. *Journal of Nursing Administration, 34*(11), 502-511. doi:10.1097/00005110-200411000-00006

Morrison, K. B., & Korol, S. A. (2014). Nurses' perceived and actual caregiving roles: identifying factors that can contribute to job satisfaction. *Journal Of Clinical Nursing, 23*(23/24), 3468-3477. doi:10.1111/jocn.12597

Moustakas, C. (1994). *Phenomenological Research Methods*. Thousand Oaks, CA: Sage Publications.

Murray, B. (2003). Qualitative research interviews: Therapeutic benefits for the participants. *Journal of Psychiatric and Mental Health Nursing, 10*(2), 233-236. doi:10.1046/j.1365-2850.2003.00553.x

National Center for PTSD (2015). *Partners of veterans with PTSD: Common problems.* Retrieved from http://www.ptsd.va.gov

National Center for PTSD. (2015). *Avoidance.* Retrieved from http://www.ptsd.va.gov

National Center for PTSD. (2015). *PTSD and problems with alcohol use.* Retrieved from http://www.ptsd.va.gov

Nayback, A. M. (2009). PTSD in the combat veteran: Using Roy's adaptation model to examine the combat veteran as a human adaptive system. *Issues in Mental Health Nursing, 30*(8), 304-310. doi:10.1080/01612840902754404

Neuman, W. L. (2003). *Social research methods* (5th ed.). Upper Saddle River, NJ: Prentice Hall.

Neuman, W. L. (2006). *Social research methods: Qualitative and quantitative approaches* (6th ed.). Boston, MA: Allyn & Bacon.

Newman, E., & Kaloupek, D. (2009). Overview of research addressing ethical dimensions of participation in traumatic stress studies: Autonomy and beneficence. *Journal Of Traumatic Stress, 22*(6), 595–602. doi:10.1002/jts.20465

Noy, C. (2008). Sampling knowledge: The hermeneutics of snowball sampling in qualitative research. *International Journal of Social Research Methodology, 11*(4), 327–344.doi:10.1080/13645570701401305

Ordin, Y. S., Karayurt, Ö., & Wellard, S. (2013). Investigation of adaptation after liver transplantation using Roy's Adaptation Model. *Nursing & Health Sciences, 15*(1), 31-38. doi:10.1111/j.1442-2018.2012.00715.x

Pacella, M. L., Hruska, B., & Delahanty, D. L. (2013). The physical health consequences of PTSD and PTSD symptoms: A meta-analytic review. *Journal of Anxiety Disorders, 27*(1), 33–46. doi:10.1016/j.janxdis.2012.08.004

Padden, D. L., Connors, R. A., & Agazio, J. G. (2011). Stress, coping, and well-being in military spouses during deployment separation. *Western Journal of Nursing Research, 33*(2), 247–267. doi:10.1177/0193945910371319

Park, M., Chang, E. R., & You, S. (2015). Protective role of coping flexibility in PTSD and depressive symptoms following trauma. *Personality and Individual Differences, 82*(-), 102-106. doi:10.1016/j.paid.2015.03.007

Pensoneau-Conway, S. L. & Toyosaki, S. (2011). Automethodology: Tracing a home for praxis-oriented ethnography. *International Journal of Qualitative Methods, 10*(4). http://ejournals.library.ualberta.ca/

Perdrizet, G. A. (1997). Hans Selye and beyond: Responses to stress. *Cell Stress & Chaperones, 2*(4), 214-219. doi:10.1379/1466-1268

Pereira, A. (2002). Combat trauma and the diagnosis of post-traumatic stress disorder in female and male veterans. *Military Medicine, 167*(1), 23-27. Retrieved from http://search.proquest.com.contentproxy.phoenix.edu

Perrett, S. E. (2007). Review of Roy adaptation model-based qualitative research. *Nursing Science Quarterly, 20*(4), 349–356. doi:10.1177/0894318407306538

Phillips, C. A. (2011). *Bridging the gap between posttraumatic stress disorder and the learning process: A phenomenological study* (Doctoral dissertation). Retrieved from ProQuest Dissertations And Theses Database. (Order No. 3480395).

Pietrzak, R. H., Goldstein, R. B., Southwick, S.M., & Grant, B. F. (2011). Prevalence and Axis I comorbidity of full and partial posttraumatic stress disorder in the United States: Results from wave 2 of the National epidemiologic survey on alcohol and related conditions. *Journal of Anxiety Disorders, 25*(3), 456–465. doi:10.1016/j.janxdis.2010.11.010

Polit, D. F., & Beck, C. T. (2004). *Nursing research: Principles and methods* (7th ed.). Philadelphia, PA: Lippincott.

Pols, H., & Oak, S. (2007). WAR and military mental health. American Journal of Public Health, 97(12), 2132–2142. doi:10.2105/AJPH.2006.090910

Ponsford, J., Kelly, A. & Couchman, G. (2014). Self-concept and self-esteem after acquired brain injury: A control group comparison. Brain Injury, 28(2), 146-154. doi:10.3109/02699052.2013.859733

Power, J. A. (2013). Courage and medical innovation : The nurses of World War One. British Journal of Nursing, 22(22). doi:10.12968/bjon.2013.22.22.1323

Ray, S. L. & Vanstone, M. (2009). The impact of PTSD on veterans' family

 relationships: An interpretative phenomenological inquiry. *International Journal*

 of Nursing Studies, 48, 38-847. doi:10.1016/j.ijnurstu.2009.01.002

Regehr C., & Bober, T. (2005). In the line of fire: Trauma in the emergency services.

 New York, NY: Oxford University Press.

Roy, C., Sr. (1988). An explication of the philosophical assumptions of the Roy

 adaptation model. *Nursing Science Quarterly, 1*(1), 26-34.

 doi:10.1177/089431848800100108

Roy, C., Sr. (2009). *The Roy adaptation model* (3rd ed.). Upper Saddle River, NJ:

 Pearson.

Roy, C., Sr. (2011a). Extending the Roy adaptation model to meet changing global needs.

 Nursing Science Quarterly 24(4), 345-351. doi:10.1177/0894318411419210

Roy, C., Sr. (2011b). Research based on the Roy adaptation model: Last 25 years.

 Nursing Science Quarterly 24(4), 312-321. doi:10.1177/0894318411419218

Sandweiss, D. A., Slymen, D. J., LeardMann, C. A., Smith, B., White, M. R., Boyko, E.

 J., . . . Smith, T. C. (2011). Preinjury psychiatric status, injury severity, and

 postdeployment posttraumatic stress disorder. *Archive of General Psychiatry,*

 68(5), 496-504. doi:10.1001/archgenpsychiatry.2011.44

Schmied, E. A., Padilla, G. A., Thomsen, C. J., Lauby, M. D. H., Harris, E., & Taylor, M.

 K. (2015). Sex differences in coping strategies in military survival school. *Journal*

 of Anxiety Disorders, 29, 7–13. doi.org/10.1016/j.janxdis.2014.10.005

Schreier, M. (2012). *Qualitative content analysis in practice*. Thousand Oaks, CA: Sage

 Publications.

Schwandt, T. A. (2007). *Dictionary of qualitative inquiry* (3rd ed.). Thousand Oaks, CA: Sage Publications.

Seal, K. H., Metzler, T., Gima, K., Bertenthal, D., Maguen, S., & Marmar, C. R. (2009). Trends and risk factors for mental health diagnoses among Iraq and Afghanistan veterans using Department of Veterans Affairs health care, 2002-2008. *American Journal of Public Health, 99*(9), 1651-1658. doi:10.2105/AJPH.2008.150284

Seedat, S. (2012). Interventions to improve psychological functioning and health outcomes of HIV-infected individuals with a history of trauma or PTSD. *Current HIV/AIDS Reports, 9*(4), 344-350. doi:10.1007/s11904-012-0139-3

Shenton, A. (2004). Strategies for ensuring trustworthiness in qualitative research projects. *Education for Information, 22*(2),* p. 63-75. Retrieved from http://web.a.ebscohost.com.contentproxy.phoenix.edu

Slaninova, G. & Stainerova, M. (2015). *Procedia-Social and Behavioral Sciences, 171,* 257-262, doi:10.1016/j.sbspro.2015.01.119

Stake, R. E. (2010). Qualitative research: Studying how things work. New York, NY: The Guilford Press.

Strauss, A., & Corbin, J. (2008). *Basics of qualitative research: Grounded theory procedures and techniques.* Thousand Oaks, CA: Sage Publications.

Streb, C. K. (2010). Exploratory case study: *Encyclopedia of case study research*, 373-375. doi.org/10.4135/9781412957397.

Tanielian, T., & Jaycox, L. (Eds.). (2008). *Invisible wounds of war: Psychological and cognitive injuries, their consequences, and services to assist recovery.* Santa Monica, CA: RAND.

Thompson, B. L., & Waltz, J. (2008). Self-compassion and PTSD symptom severity. *Journal of Traumatic Stress*, *21*(6), 556-558. doi:10.1002/jts.20374

Tiet, Q. Q., Rosen, C., Cavella, S., Moos, R. H., Finney, J. W., & Yesavage, J. (2006). Coping, symptoms, and functioning outcomes of patients with posttraumatic stress disorder. *Journal Of Traumatic Stress*, *19*(6), 799–811. doi.org/10.1002/jts.20185 live

Tsai, J., Harpaz-Rotem, I., Pietrzak, R. H., & Southwick, S. M. (2012). The role of coping, resilience, and social support in mediating the relation between PTSD and social functioning in veterans returning from Iraq and Afghanistan. *Psychiatry*, *75*(2), 135–149. doi.org/10.1521/psyc.2012.75.2.135

Tural, U., Onder, E., & Aker, T. (2012). Effect of depression on recovery from PTSD. *Community Mental Health Journal, 48*(2), 161–166. doi:10.1007/s10597-010-9359-4

U.S. Army. (2010). Army health promotion risk reduction suicide prevention. Washington, D.C.: U.S. Army Publishing Directorate.

U.S. Department of Veterans Affairs. (2014). *DSM-5 diagnostic criteria for PTSD released*. Washington, D.C. Retrieved from http://www.ptsd.va.gov/professional/PTSD-overview

Ursano, R. J., Fullerton, C. S., Weisaeth, L., & Raphael, B. (Eds.). (2007). *Textbook of disaster psychiatry*. New York, NY: Cambridge.

Utsey, S. O., Bolden, M. A., Lanier, Y., & Williams, O. (2007). Examining the role of culture-specific coping as a predictor of resilient outcomes in African Americans from high-risk urban communities. *Journal of Black Psychology, 33*(1), 75-93. doi:10.1177/0095798406295094

Veenstra, M. Y., Lemmens, P. H. H. M., Friesema, I. H. M., Tan, F. E. S., Garretsen H. F. L., Knottnerus, J. A. & Zwietering, P. J. (2007). Coping style mediates impact of stress on alcohol use: A prospective population-based study. *Addiction, 102*(12), 1890-1898. doi.010.1111/j.1360-0443.2007.02026.x

Vivar, C. G., McQueen, A., Whyte, D. A., & Armayor, N. C. (2007). Getting started with qualitative research: developing a research proposal. *Nurse Researcher, 14*(3), 60-73. doi:/10.7748/nr2007.04.14.3.60.c6033

Walker, J. L. (2012). The use of saturation in qualitative research. *Canadian Journal of Cardiovascular Nursing - Journal Canadien En Soins Infirmiers Cardio-Vasculaires, 22*(2), 37-46. doi.org/10.1007/s11747-007-0077-6

Warden, D. (2006). Military TBI during the Iraq and Afghanistan wars. *Journal of Head Trauma Rehabilitation, 21*(5), 23-25. doi:10.1097/00001199-200609000-00004.

Weidlich, C. P., & Ugarriza, Doris N. (2015). A pilot study examining the impact of care provider support program on resiliency, coping, and compassion fatigue in military health care providers. *Military Medicine, 180*(3), 290-295. Retrieved from http://search.proquest.com

West, I. (n. d.). *The women of the Army Nurse Corps during the Vietnam War*. Retrieved from Vietnam Women's Memorial Foundation website: http://www.vietnamwomensmemorial.org

Westhuis, D. J., Fafara, R. J., & Ouellette, P. (2006). Does ethnicity affect the coping of military spouses? *Armed Forces & Society, 32*, 584-603. doi.org/10.1177/0095327X06287050

Wilgus, K. A. (2011). Off to Afghanistan: Nursing in a combat zone. *Nurse Educator, 36*(6), 238-240. doi:10.1097/NNE.0b013e3182333cb8

Wilkins, K. C., Lang, A. J., & Norman, S. B. (2011). Synthesis of the psychometric properties of the PTSD checklist (PCL) military, civilian, and specific versions. *Depression & Anxiety 28*(7), 596–606. doi.org/10.1002/da.20837

Yin, R. K. (2009). *Case study research: Design and methods* (4th ed.). Thousand Oaks, CA: Sage Publications.

Yin, R. K. (2012). *Applications of case study research* (3rd ed.). Thousand Oaks, CA: Sage Publications.

Appendix A

Permission for Content Analysis

S. Elo and H. Kyngäs

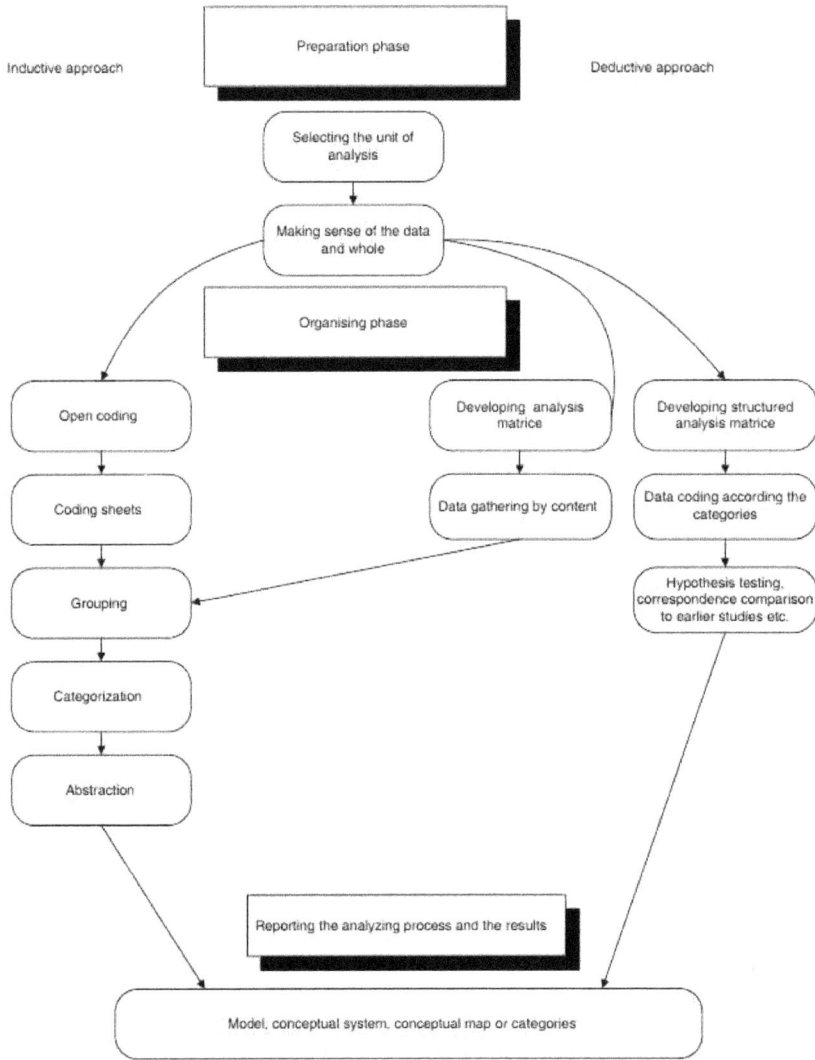

Figure 1 Preparation, organizing and resulting phases in the content analysis process.

172

Appendix B

Permission for Human Adaptive System Diagram

Appendix C

Permission for Roy Middle-Range Theory

Boston College
William F. Connell School of Nursing

December 16, 2015

To: ███████

From: Sr. Callista Roy, PhD, RN, FAAN

Re: Letter of Permission

To whom it may concern,

This letter provides ███████ permission to use the Middle-Range Theory of Coping and Adaptation Processing figure for her doctoral thesis and all follow up work. This permission extends to all educational, practice and research endeavors. It omits any permission for proprietary purposes.

I wish you well in your continuing contributions to nursing.

Sincerely,

Sr. Callista Roy, PhD, RN, FAAN
Professor and Nurse Theorist

Appendix D

Demographic Questionnaire

THANK YOU FOR TAKING THE TIME TO ACCESS THIS QUESTIONNAIRE. PLEASE ANSWER <u>ALL QUESTION</u>

*   1. Name:

*   2. What is your preferred method of contact

*   3. What is the best time to contact you?

*   4. Please select your age range

*   5. Do you read, write, and speak English?

*   6. Are you cognitively impaired?

*   7. Are you male or female?

        8. What is your ethnicity? (Please select all that apply.)

*   9. Do you live within 30 miles of _____

*   10. Are you a veteran registered nurse?

*   11. Please select your branch of service

*   12. Which of the following categories best describe your current status?

☐ Active duty

☐ Separated *(fulfilled obligation)*

☐ Retired *(regular and/or disability)*

*   13. To what area were you deployed?

*   14. What conflict(s) did you deploy in support of? *(Choose all that apply)*

*   15. Were you medically diagnosed with combat related PTSD?

*   16. Are you willing to discuss your experiences and your coping and

adaptation

*   strategies in an interview

Appendix E

Military Version of PTSD Checklist (PCL-M)

Participant's Name:_____Date:_____

Branch of Service_____Rank:_____

INSTRUCTIONS: Below is a list of problems and complaints that veterans sometimes have in response to stressful military experiences. Please read each one carefully, then put and **"X"** in the box the right to indicate how much you have been bothered by that problem <u>in the past month.</u> *Respond as you did when you were first diagnosed with PTSD.*

Problem or Complaint	Not at all	A little bit	Moderately	Quite a bit	Extremely
	1	2	3	4	5
1. Repeated, disturbing memories, thoughts, or images of a stressful military experience?					
2. Repeated, disturbing dreams of a stressful military experience?					
3. Suddenly acting or feeling as if a stressful military experience were happening again (as if you were reliving it)?					
4. Feeling very upset when something reminded you of a stressful military experience?					
5. Having physical reactions (e.g., heart pounding, trouble breathing, sweating) when something reminded you of a stressful military experience?					
6. Avoiding thinking about or talking about a stressful military experience or avoiding having feelings related to it?					
7. Avoiding activities or situations because they reminded you of a stressful military experience?					
8. Trouble remembering important parts of a stressful military experience?					
9. Loss of interest in activities that you used to enjoy?					
10. Feeling distant or cut off from other people?					
11. Feeling emotionally numb or being unable to have loving feelings for those close to you?					
12. Feeling as if your future will somehow be cut short?					
13. Trouble falling or staying asleep?					
14. Feeling irritable or having angry outbursts?					
15. Having difficulty concentrating?					
16. Being "super-alert" or watchful or on guard?					
17. Feeling jumpy or easily startled?					

Appendix F

Interview Questions

Date:_____

Interview Start Time_____   Interview End Time:_____

1. What symptoms of PTSD, if any, have you recognized in yourself? When did you first notice these symptoms?

2. How have these symptoms affected your performance, if at all, and are you doing anything to address the changes in your performance?

3. How have you coped with and adapted to PTSD?

4. In terms of experiencing PTSD, what do coping and adapting mean and what does it involve?

5. How does having PTSD affect your view of yourself? Why?

6. How does having PTSD affect your relationships with others? Why?

Closing
Do you wish to share any final comments about coping and adaptation? Thank you for your cooperation and participation. If you have additional questions or concerns, please feel free to call me or send me an email. Thank you for taking the time to meet with me.

Appendix G

Confidentiality Agreement

University of Phoenix

EXPLORING COPING AND ADAPTATION IN VETERAN ARMY NURSES WITH
COMBAT-RELATED POST-TRAUMATIC STRESS DISORDER COPING AND

Confidentiality Agreement

As a researcher working on the aforementioned research study at the University of
Phoenix, I understand that I must maintain the confidentiality of all information concerning all
research participants as required by law. Only the University of Phoenix Institutional Review
Board may have access to this information. "Confidential Information" of participants includes
but is not limited to: names, characteristics, or other identifying information, questionnaire
scores, ratings, incidental comments, other information accrued either directly or indirectly
through contact with any participant, and/or any other information that by its nature would be
considered confidential. In order to maintain the confidentiality of the information, I hereby
agree to refrain from discussing or disclosing any Confidential Information regarding research
participants, to any individual who is not part of the above research study or in need of the
information for the expressed purposes on the research program. This includes having a
conversation regarding the research project or its participants in a place where such a discussion
might be overheard; or discussing any Confidential Information in a way that would allow an
unauthorized person to associate (either correctly or incorrectly) an identity with such
information. I further agree to store research records whether paper, electronic or otherwise in a
secure locked location under my direct control or with appropriate safe guards. I hereby further
agree that if I have to use the services of a third party to assist in the research study, who will
potentially have access to any Confidential Information of participants, that I will enter into an
agreement with said third party prior to using any of the services, which shall provide at a
minimum the confidential obligations set forth herein. I agree that I will immediately report any
known or suspected breach of this confidentiality statement regarding the above research project
to the University of Phoenix, Institutional Review Board.

Signature of Researcher

Signature of Witness

178

Appendix H

Personal Journaling Sample

I feel very strange acting in the role of interviewer because of my intimate relationship with PTSD. Hearing the experience of_____made me realize that some common threads of coping can be found in almost everyone. I tell myself I need to be patient and focus, and allow the data to unveil and to lift from the pages of the interviews and from the dialogue of the interviews. I didn't tell anyone that I was diagnosed with PTSD and I'm wondering if this makes me a fake. Should I tell them? If I do, will it influence their responses? In order for me to get unbiased and honest answers, and to protect the integrity of the study. I have decided not to disclose my affinity with the topic of PTSD. After this interview I asked myself if my research will be useful to anyone. My response to the question is who is to judge the usefulness of this study?

Appendix I

Letter of Support

Appendix K

Recruitment Flyer

VOLUNTEERS NEEDED FOR A RESEARCH STUDY
EXPLORING <u>COPING AND ADAPTATION</u> IN ARMY
NURSES WITH COMBAT-RELATED <u>PTSD</u>

- Are you an Active Duty, Retired OR Separated Army Registered Nurse?
- Have you been deployed at least once in support of OIF/OEF/OND?
- Have you been diagnosed with PTSD?

If you answered <u>**YES**</u> to <u>**ALL**</u> three questions, you may be eligible to participate in this research study.

The purpose of the study is to examine how Army nurses with combat-related PTSD are coping and adapting. **There are NO financial or personal benefits to participants,** but the study results may benefit Military Nurses in general.

Both male and female Army RNs are eligible to participate. **Time commitment will range from 45-60 minutes per interview.** The study is being conducted by ███████ ██████████

If you are interested, please contact ███████████ at (—) — - —- or _____@gmail.com for more information.

@gmail.com	@gmail.com	@gmail.com	@gmail.com	@gmail.com	@gmail.com	@gmail.com	@gmail.com	@gmail.com

Appendix L

Letter of Introduction

University of Phoenix®

Dear:

Thank you for your interest in *EXPLORING COPING AND ADAPTATION OF VETERAN ARMY NURSES WITH COMBAT-RELATED POST-TRAUMATIC STRESS DISORDER.* I am a student at University of Phoenix in the School of Advanced Studies. The purpose of this qualitative case study is to explore how army nurses diagnosed with combat-related PTSD cope and adapt. It is my hope that data gathered from this study may contribute to nurses discovering unknown strengths and weaknesses about themselves that may significantly affect the nursing population. Additionally, the findings may lead to the development and implementation of strategies to provide specialized mental health services to army nurses and the general population who may be experiencing PTSD.

The study will involve face-to-face interviews conducted in a private room at the local library. Your time commitment is 45–60 minutes per interview. If you choose to participate, you will be required to sign a consent form before any interview is done. After signing the consent form, I will provide you with the address of a secure website where you can access a demographic questionnaire for you to complete. Your identity will be protected throughout the study and your information will be secured. Again, thank you for your interest in this study. If you need further information you may contact me at the number below.

Sincerely,

Appendix M

Permission to Use Library

- Permission to Use Premises

Please complete the following by check marking any permissions that you grant. Also, please provide your signature, title, date, and organizational information below. If you have any questions or concerns about this research study, please contact the University of Phoenix Institutional Review Board via email at IRB@phoenix.edu.

☒I hereby authorize ▮▮▮▮▮▮▮▮, a student of University of Phoenix, to use the premises (facility identified below) to conduct a study entitled *Coping and Adaptation of Veteran Army Nurses with Combat-Related Post-Traumatic Stress Disorder.*

▮▮▮▮▮▮▮▮▮▮   ▮▮▮▮▮▮▮
Signature   Date

▮▮▮▮▮▮▮▮
Name

▮▮▮▮▮▮▮▮
Title

▮▮▮▮▮▮
Address of Facility

184

Appendix N

Consent Form

University of Phoenix®

INFORMED CONSENT: PARTICIPANTS 18 YEARS OF AGE AND OLDER

Dear Participant,

My name is_____and I am a student at the University of Phoenix working on a PhD degree in nursing. I am doing a research study entitled *Coping and Adaptation of Veteran Army Nurses with Combat-related Post-Traumatic Stress Disorder*. The purpose of the research study is to explore how army nurses with combat-related PTSD are coping and adapting.

VOLUNTARY PARTICIPATION

You are being asked to consider participation in this research study, which will involve being interviewed for no more than 45 to 60 minutes. The decision to participate in this study is completely voluntary on your part. You may withdraw consent at any time and discontinue further participation in this study without any penalty. Should you choose to withdraw, you must notify the Researcher immediately. Upon notification, a certified letter acknowledging your withdrawal will be mailed to you.

If you withdraw and request to withdraw your data, all research materials and data related to you will be immediately destroyed. Data collected prior to withdrawal from the study will become part of the study record and will be retained to protect the scientific validity of the study. If any portion of this data is used in the final dissertation or in material submitted for publication, your confidentiality and anonymity will be maintained. The Researcher of this study may terminate your participation in the study at any time if she feels this to be in your best interest.

RISKS OR DISCOMFORTS

You may experience some minor emotional discomfort while responding to the research questions. If you become upset at any time while answering any question, you may stop the interview and resume at a later date or you may choose to not continue with the interview. I acknowledge that you are agreeing to spend your time and share personal information, which you might not otherwise do. A licensed counselor will be on call by phone during the interview hours to assist you if you experience any emotional discomfort. The counselor will be available within 5 minutes of the call. It is possible that breach of confidentiality may also be a risk for study participants who are in active duty status, because information regarding your health may be required to be reported to

185

appropriate medical or command authorities. There may be other unforeseen risks associated with this study.

ENTITLEMENT TO CARE
In the event of injury resulting from this study, the extent of medical care provided is limited and will be within the scope authorized for Department of Defense (DoD) health care beneficiaries. Federal laws and regulations govern your entitlement to medical and dental care and/or compensation in the event of injury. If you have questions about your rights as a research subject, you may contact The University of Phoenix Institutional Review Board for the Protection of Human Subjects at (480) 557-3049 or email: IRB@phoenix.edu

CONFIDENTIALITY OF STUDY PARTICIPANTS
By signing this consent document, you give your permission for information gained from your participation in this study to be published in the relevant literature, and used generally to further nursing and medical science. You will not be personally identified; all information will be presented as anonymous to protect you.

Complete confidentiality cannot be promised for active duty military personnel, because information regarding your health may be required to be reported to appropriate medical or command authorities. Confidential information may be disclosed to an appropriate medical or behavioral health professional if your responses to any question indicate a potential for self-harm or serious medical or behavioral risk.

DATA SECURITY
As a participant in this study, you should understand that data would be kept for a minimum of three years in a secured, double-locked area at the Researcher's home and then destroyed. It is necessary to record interviews and as such, your permission is required for the Researcher,_____, to record the interviews. You understand that the information from the recorded interviews will be transcribed. The Researcher will use a computer generated alphanumeric code to identify data, and pseudonyms will be used to report data results to ensure your protection.

BENEFITS
There are no benefits associated with your participation in this study other than knowing that the study results may help current and/or future research on studies involving army nurses who are coping and adapting with PTSD.

CONTACT INFORMATION

You are encouraged to ask any questions, at any time that will help you to understand how this study will be performed and/or how it will affect you. You may contact me at

_____

ACKNOWLEDGEMENT

By signing this form, you agree that you understand the nature of the study, the possible risks to you as a participant, and how your identity will be kept confidential. If you sign this form you are acknowledging that you are 18 years old or older and that you give your permission to volunteer as a participant in the study that is described here. A signed and dated copy of this form will be given to you for your records

(☐) I accept the above terms. (☐) I do not accept the above terms. (CHECK ONE)

Signature of Participant_____Date _____

Signature of Researcher_____Date _____

Appendix O

Non-Disclosure Agreement

_____, LCSW, acknowledges that in order to provide the services to ███████ (hereinafter "Researcher") who is a researcher in a confidential study with the University of Phoenix, Inc. _____ must agree to keep the information obtained as part of her services (as more fully described below) confidential. Therefore the parties agree as follows:

1. The information to be disclosed under this Nondisclosure Agreement ("Agreement") is described as follows and shall be considered "Confidential Information": in providing any counseling needed for the participants. All protected health information inclusive of, but not limited to names, characteristics, or other identifying information, questionnaires, scores, ratings, incidental comments, other information accrued either directly or indirectly through contact with any participant, and/or any other information that by its nature would be considered confidential. All information shall remain the property of Researcher.

2. _____ agrees to keep in confidence and to use the Confidential Information for *counseling* only and for no other purposes.
3. _____ further agrees to keep in confidence and not disclose any Confidential Information to a third party or parties for a period of five (5) years from the date of such disclosure. All oral disclosures of Confidential Information as well as written disclosures of the Confidential Information are covered by this Agreement.
4. _____ shall upon Researcher's request either destroy or return the Confidential Information upon termination of this Agreement.
5. Any obligation of _____ under this Agreement shall not apply to Confidential Information that:
6. Is or becomes a part of the public knowledge through no fault of hers.
7. _____ can demonstrate was rightfully in her possession before disclosure by Researcher/ research subjects; or
8. _____ can demonstrate was rightfully received from a third party who was not Researcher/research subjects and was not under confidentiality restriction on disclosure and without breach of any nondisclosure obligation.
9. _____ shall defend, indemnify and hold the Researcher and the University of Phoenix harmless against any third party claims of damage or injury of any kind resulting from _____ use of the Confidential Information, or any violation of by _____ of the terms of this Agreement.
10. In the event _____ receives a subpoena and believes she has a legal obligation to disclose Confidential Information, then _____ will notify Researcher as soon as possible, and in any event at least five (5) business days prior to the proposed release. If Researcher objects to the release of such Confidential Information, _____ will allow Researcher to exercise any legal rights or remedies regarding the release and protection of the Confidential Information.
11. _____ expressly acknowledges and agrees that the breach, or threatened breach, through a disclosure of Confidential Information may cause irreparable harm and that Researcher may not have an adequate remedy at law. Therefore, _____ agrees that upon such breach, or threatened breach, Researcher will be entitled to seek injunctive

relief to prevent _____ from commencing or continuing any action constituting such breach without showing or providing evidence of actual damage.

The interpretation and validity of this Agreement and the rights of the parties shall be governed by the laws of the State of Texas.

The parties to this Agreement agree that a copy of the original signature (including an electronic copy) may be used for any and all purposes for which the original signature may have been used. The parties further waive any right to challenge the admissibility or authenticity of this document in a court of law based solely on the absence of an original signature.

IN WITNESS WHEREOF, each of the undersigned has caused this Agreement to be duly executed in their names and on their behalf:

Printed Name of Licensed Counselor: _____

Signature: _____

Address: _____

Date: _____

Printed Name of Researchers _____

Signature: _____

Address: _____

Date: _____

Appendix P

Letter of Instructions to Participant

Dear:

I want to thank you again for your willingness to participate in the research study of *Coping and Adaptation of Army Nurses with Combat-related PTSD.* Attached is a transcript of your interview. Please review it for accuracy. If you have any concerns, corrections, or would like to clarify any of the information in the transcript, please annotate them in the right margin of the transcript in red ink. Then, return the complete transcript with a signed copy of this letter in the enclosed self- addressed stamped envelope within 5 days.

By signing this letter in ink, I acknowledge that I received a copy of the transcript of my interview with instructions, and that I understand the instructions provided to me. I also understand that the transcripts with a signed copy of this letter must be returned within 5 days
using the self-addressed stamped envelope.

_____

Name (please print legibly)

_____   _____

Signature   Date

AB ASPECT Books

We invite you to view the complete
selection of titles we publish at:
www.ASPECTBooks.com

We encourage you to write us
with your thoughts about this,
or any other book we publish at:
info@ASPECTBooks.com

ASPECT Books' titles may be purchased in
bulk quantities for educational, fund-raising,
business, or promotional use.
bulksales@ASPECTBooks.com

Finally, if you are interested in seeing
your own book in print, please contact us at:
publishing@ASPECTBooks.com

We are happy to review your manuscript at no charge.

www.ingramcontent.com/pod-product-compliance
Lightning Source LLC
Chambersburg PA
CBHW061757260326
41914CB00006B/1143